FLIGHT

TO A

LADY

The story of Arthur Butler's record-breaking flight from England to Australia in 1931

by

C. Arthur Butler

First printed 2007.

Reprinted 2008 and 2017.

© C. Arthur Butler 2017

ISBN 978-0-646-48244-6

C. Arthur Butler in cockpit of Comper Swift.

Foreword

Nancy Bird, A.O., O.B.E., Hon.D.Sc., Hon.M.E.

I had the privilege of reading this manuscript whilst Arthur was still alive so I am delighted that this story of blood, sweat and tears of early aviation has been published.

Arthur Butler got his inspiration for aviation one day when sitting under a large pine tree and a pine cone on the tree above expelled its seeds which floated to the ground. Capturing one of the seeds he observed it was a natural example of aerodynamics and this led him to see the possibilities of flight and created his desire to fly.

Arthur went to Mascot, got a job, lived very frugally and at night attended free lectures at the Technical College after his day's work. He won 25 pounds for a paper he wrote which gave him the fare to Melbourne where he got a job with a pioneer aviation company. He worked long hours and eventually bought a crashed aeroplane which he started rebuilding in his spare time after work and would often continue until the early hours of the morning.

He used to taxi his aeroplane back and forth across the airfield to get the feel of the aircraft to see if it would fly. One morning at 7.30 a.m. he was running late for work so whilst he was taxiing across the airfield he opened the throttle a bit more and the plane took off! That was Arthur's first solo flight.

He built up an aviation company and put Cootamundra on the map aviation wise until he was ruthlessly taken over by Reg Ansett who gave one hundred of his staff one share in Butler's company and sent them to Sydney to vote him out of his own company at a general meeting in Sydney.

I was privileged to travel around the country with him raising money which put the first air ambulance in the air by public subscription.

Arthur Butler's name will live on in aviation history and I congratulate the Cootamundra Council on naming its terminal in his memory.

Aviation history would not be complete without Arthur Butler's history.

Nancy Bird

Nancy Bird
September 2007

Introduction

C. Arthur Butler was a pioneer aviator who in the early days of flying in Australia introduced the aeroplane and the joy and excitement of flying to many isolated communities.

In his barnstorming days he visited over 200 places in NSW beside areas of Queensland and Tasmania. He landed in any spot that afforded enough room for a landing and takeoff which meant any road or paddock that did not have many obstacles such as livestock or people.

It was during one of his barnstorming trips that he met my mother whose family lived at Tooraweenah a small town near the foot of the Warrumbungle Mountains. He became a regular visitor landing his plane on the road outside her home.

During this period father had designed and was building his own plane which he hoped to fly to England and perhaps find a market for it. Unfortunately it did not pass the stringent test required for such a long journey, so he decided to go to England by ship to see what aviation design positions were available, as there were far more opportunities overseas.

The account of his adventures in England and his meeting with Nicholas Comper and the extraordinary flight which was the outcome of their meeting is the record of what must be one of the most courageous and quixotic journeys ever undertaken in aviation history. This record-breaking flight in the tiny Comper Swift took 9 days 1 hour and 43 minutes. It is the smallest open plane to have made this journey and the record still holds to this day.

My father married my mother four months after his return to Australia. Eventually he formed Butler Air Transport which pioneered many air routes in rural NSW and brought a much- needed service to isolated country communities.

Butler Airtransport began operation in 1934 in Cootamundra serving the mail route between Cootamundra and Charleville. This formed a section of the Empire Airmail linking Australia and Great Britain. This service ran until 1938 when the company transferred to Sydney. The main reason for this was the Empire Airmail Service planes were superceded by flying boats which flew into Sydney.

Butler Airtransport was granted a contract to fly airmail from Sydney to outback rural areas which included Mendooran, Tooraweenah, Coonamble, Brewarrina and Bourke. The airmail service eventually extended into a passenger service using Dragon Rapides and later DC3s and finally Viscounts.

During the war Butler Airtransport was engaged in manufacturing wooden aircraft parts and also metal components for Mosquitos.

The company did this work for no profit, the Government covering the cost for parts only. The company also organised parties which flew to R.A.A.F. stations in the country to entertain troops at weekends.

The company ran most successfully until 1958 when it was taken over by Ansett Airways. This was an enormous blow to my father who was only 56 and still full of ideas and energy. However, through his forced retirement he found new avenues of interest. He took up painting and was successful in having his entry in the Winn Landscape prize hung at the Art Gallery of NSW.

He also wrote a history of Civil Aviation in Australia and parts one and two of his memoirs, part two being *Flight to a Lady*.

We hope that this volume will fill an important part of aviation history besides being an interesting and enjoyable read.

Anna Yeats
October 2007

Flight To A Lady

Long ago a very good friend of mine fell in love. A charming, sane intelligent companion who suddenly became a tiresome bore with thoughts and conversation centred on nought but the virtues of a mere woman. Appalled by the drastic change in the character of my friend I fervently hoped to be forever spared the affliction of this demoralizing malady.

Many years went by, leaving me immune to the allurements of the fair sex. Then without warning I fell in love with a lovely lady whose indescribable charm thoroughly bewildered me. Terrified I fled the country, hoping distance would allay the startling sensation which had beset me.

Arriving in England at the end of summer 1931, with hope of continuing my career in aviation, I was fortunate to obtain a position in the design office of Saunders-Roe, Cowes, Isle of Wight thanks to Mr. HE. Broadsmith, the Managing Director, who had given me my start in aviation ten years previously, after establishing the first aircraft factory in Australia.

I was due to join Saunders-Roe in November, when the company started work on a flying boat contract it had obtained from the British Government. With letters of introduction to several other aircraft manufacturers, I decided to visit as many of these as possible, during the intervening period.

At the beginning of 'the thirties' aviation was on the threshold of a new era. A time when the aircraft industry was seriously applying itself to designing and producing commercial aircraft capable of economic operation without the aid of subsidy, thus providing tremendous opportunities for people like myself to reach great heights in this profession. A fact I realised fully when I set out on 7th October, to visit the Hawker Sopwith works at Kingston on Thames.

After spending the day at Kingston on Thames, where the Fury fighter was being produced, I stayed the night in London, intending to visit the Vickers works at Brooklands, near Weybridge on the following day. On my way to Brooklands I collected my mail from Australia House, then strolled along to Strand station intending to take the underground to Waterloo, thence by train to Weybridge.

At the Strand, instead of boarding a south bound train, acting on a sudden and illogical impulse I took a northbound train for Euston, where I sent a telegram to an uncle living near Birkenhead, accepting a standing invitation to spend a few days with him.

Less than an hour later I was on a Liverpool bound train gazing at the beauty of rural England unfolding before me, entirely unaware that I had embarked on an adventure which would change the whole course of my life.

Although I had planned to visit my uncle and aunt before settling down to work, I had no urgent desire to see these kinsfolk who were strangers to me. Such irrational behaviour puzzled me so much that the train had passed through Rugby before I realised I had forgotten to look at my mail from Australia, which included a letter from a country friend containing news that the young lady who had so entranced me was being ardently courted by a local grazier. Disturbing news which caused me to do some mental stocktaking.

Prior to becoming enamoured, I had enjoyed life immensely by concentrating the whole of my mental and physical energies on acquiring as much skill and knowledge as possible since the time I had first become attracted to aviation. The possibility of my career being jeopardised because of my amorous distraction had impelled me to get away from the cause.

I told myself 'This is only a passing infatuation which would fade to a pleasant memory by the time I reached England'. Yet, despite the wonderful places I had seen enroute, the attraction of my new environment and contemplation of my excellent prospects with Saunders-Roe, my uppermost thoughts were still centred on the lady from whom I'd fled, more than three months ago.

The idea of the lady being married to someone else set my mind in such a turmoil. I arrived at my destination looking so miserable my uncle assumed the English climate did not agree with me. He, like many others I met later, was under the impression that the Australian climate was akin to that of Hades.

Coming from such a torrid place to Cheshire - which was experiencing the coldest October for over 50 years - was enough to endanger the life of any 'colonial from the antipodes' according to my uncle, who seemed rather fond of Edwardian expressions.

My aunt's opinion was entirely different. She said I looked half starved and needed a few decent meals to make a man of me. A comment I didn't like, nor did I appreciate my aunt's reaction when I was unable to eat the excellent dinner she provided that evening. Convinced I was suffering from something more serious than malnutrition my aunt questioned me relentlessly about my recent movements, my habits, where and what food I had eaten recently.

The inquisition ended with my aunt administering a large dose of licorice powder and my being put to bed with a hot water bottle provided by my uncle. These remedies did nothing towards relieving my miserable mental state, although the licorice powder created a somewhat startling situation in the early hours of the following morning.

My uncle and aunt lived at Higher Bebbington, a Cheshire village about 5 miles from Birkenhead - rapidly losing its rural atmosphere to invading Lancastrian urbanity. They were middle class, a term used by my uncle, who referred to this vague stratum of English society as the backbone of

Britain. 'A backbone slightly dislocated by that socialist Ramsay Macdonald and his crackpot ideas', quoted my uncle, a staunch conservative.

Other than politics, my father's brother showed little interest in things beyond his immediate environment. Apart from the garden which occasionally claimed his reluctant attention, his leisure was taken up by tending to and once in a while, driving an ancient, though immaculate motor car, his pride and joy.

The household was dominated by my aunt, a woman of ample proportions whose main interests in life seemed to be food, the ailments of mankind and their cure. Childless she showered her affection on two slobbering spaniels, almost as wide in girth as their mistress.

My uncle was also rotund, a state he attributed to the culinary art of his wife, who thought otherwise. In her opinion, her husband's obesity was due to lack of exercise. She had, a few weeks before my arrival, presented him with a bicycle, saying if he wished to continue sharing her bed, he must take to cycling to reduce his figure to - what my aunt termed - reasonable proportions.

After a fruitless argument, my uncle had hung the bicycle in the garage and bought himself another bed.

The domestic affairs of my relatives may seem irrelevant, indeed they would be, except had it not been for that bicycle this story would never have been written.

On the morning following the day of my arrival after listening to my uncle's waggish explanation concerning the bicycle I borrowed it and rode away to explore the countryside and work off the huge breakfast my aunt had insisted on my eating.

Cycling along the leaf strewn lanes of the Wirral on that cold but sunny morning was quite exhilarating, but my pleasure was marred by my agony of mind, debating whether I should carry on with my career in

England or succumb to my desire to woo a lady 13,000 miles away. A battle in my brain which continued unremittingly whilst my feet went round and round pushing the bicycle along mile after mile. Pausing to regain my breath after climbing a long incline I was confronted with a panorama of extraordinary beauty. The estuary of the Dee bordered by lush meadows, the hills of Wales forming a backdrop in the distance, with a few fleecy clouds floating in a pale blue sky and the variegated colour of the trees near by, completing the idyllic scene.

It was here that Britain lost one of its potential aircraft designers and a future test pilot, when unheedful of Johnson's adage, 'No wise man will quit a certainty for an uncertainty', I decided to return to Australia as soon as possible and plight my troth.

My first impulse was to rush back to Higher Bebbington, pick up my scanty belongings and head for London, taking passage from there in the first ship bound for Australia. To do this would probably subject me to another interrogation by my aunt whom I doubted had any romantic inclination. She would more than likely attribute my hasty action to some malady of the mind which could be cured by one of her sadistic remedies. Frankly, I was rather scared of my aunt.

The previous evening I had said I intended leaving on (Saturday) to visit two aunts living near Birmingham. It would be wiser to adhere to this plan, and go on to London first thing on Monday morning. After all, it was most unlikely for a ship to be sailing for Australia during the weekend.

Then I realised several days might be saved going by train to Marseille or even Naples if a homeward bound ship happened to be conveniently leaving either of these places.

Although disliking the idea of disturbing my uncle, who managed a small engineering works near Birkenhead, during business hours, I decided to enlist his aid in obtaining information about getting to Australia by the quickest means.

It is not easy to find your way in England without a map. Though the country is not lacking in signposts, these, in the main, only indicate places in the immediate vicinity.

In a dilemma about the best way to reach Birkenhead and only a hazy idea of distance and direction, I turned into a lane, hoping it would lead to the main road from Chester to Birkenhead.

The lane, too narrow for vehicles to pass, twisted and turned between high hedges which blocked out the view, so that before I had gone any distance it was impossible to judge the direction I was heading. No traffic passed that way, in fact I might well have been in the middle of the Simpson Desert except for the abounding elm and chestnut trees silently shedding their leaves on this meandering lane which seemed to be leading nowhere.

Unaware that I was fated never to reach Birkenhead I cycled along as fast as possible, until the track, ridding itself of its enclosing hedges, wound up a slope so steep I was forced to dismount.

The view from the crest was marred by haze, but the way ahead was clear enough to see the lane led to civilized parts, with possibilities of finding someone to direct me.

Soon I came to a crossroads and a signpost indicating Bromborough 6 miles. I was eleven miles from my destination. As I turned on the Bromborough road an aeroplane passed overhead, the first I had seen aloft in England.

Despite my hurry, I dismounted and watched the machine circle, its engine coughing and banging then glide out of sight beyond some trees about a mile away. Either the pilot had been forced to land or there was an aerodrome in the vicinity.

Torn between my desire to get to Birkenhead as soon as possible and the impulse to see if the airman was in trouble, I fished out my 'Boyproof ' watch. It showed twenty to two. Plenty of time remained to satisfy my curiosity and get to my uncle's office before it closed.

Within five minutes I came to an aerodrome with a number of workshops and hangars. In trouble or not the airman would have facilities at his disposal.

I was about to turn back when another aircraft circled above and came into land. The smallest aeroplane I had ever seen.

Fascinated, I watched the midget make a perfect touchdown, then mindful of my mission, remounted my bicycle and hastened away, but after travelling a few yards, an irresistible impulse compelled me to turn about and enter the aerodrome.

Going over to a spectator standing on the tarmac, I said 'Good day, Would you mind telling me what type of aircraft that is?' Indicating the small aeroplane now being taxied towards us.

Instead of replying, the man spent several seconds gazing at me and my bicycle. Then rather disdainfully asked 'You're a colonial, aren't you?'

Before I could think of a suitable retort to what seemed to me to be a stupid and impertinent question, the subject of my enquiry rolled to a standstill a few feet away.

The pilot jumped out to be casually greeted by the spectator whilst I walked around the aircraft admiring the little beauty.

Being not more than 5 feet high, less than 20 feet in length and a little more than that in wing span. Despite its size, this miniature aeroplane, so elegantly proportioned, was very attractive. The sort of aircraft that gave one the urge to fly.

After a brief conversation with his colleague, the pilot came over to me and asked. 'Well, what do you think of her?'

His cultured English voice matched that of his colleague. There the similarity ended. The pilot was a comparatively small man with dark hair and complexion, lively hazel eyes and friendly smile. A great contrast to the big, thick set, fair haired Nordic type, who had tabbed me 'Colonial'.

Evidently pleased with my reply to his enquiry, the pilot introduced himself as Nicholas Comper. It was then I remembered reading about a new type of aircraft, a Comper Swift, finishing third in the last King's Cup race. When I mentioned this, Comper nodded at the aircraft, saying 'That's the little beauty'.

For over an hour we discussed every aspect of flying in Britain and in Australia. By then there was not much Nic Comper didn't know about my activities in aviation, or I of Comper's. He had been in the R.A.F. engaged on general duties for several years, later becoming one of the 'Boffins' at the experimental base at Farnborough. He had forgone his service career and established an organisation to design and manufacture light aircraft. The Swift was the first of what he hoped would be a long line of successful types.

Suddenly remembering my mission, I reluctantly said farewell. Comper then asked 'Would you care to fly the Swift?'

I don't know who was more surprised by this invitation, Comper's colleague or I. I was certainly the first to recover, donning the cap and goggles handed to me by Comper and slipping into the cockpit before the other fellow had a chance to protest.

Seconds later, as I taxied the Swift into position for takeoff I wondered what had possessed Nicholas Comper to entrust me, a complete stranger, with his racing machine. Usually having to work very hard for anything, to be offered this flight 'on a plate' so to speak, rather astounded me.

Carefully heading the Swift into wind, I opened the throttle intent on flying this aircraft with such purpose, that Comper's confidence would be well justified and his colleague - who seemed none too pleased about the matter - nonplussed.

At rest on the ground an aeroplane is just an inanimate piece of machinery, but aloft it seems to become alive, responding to the touch of its pilot as a horse responds to handling by its rider. Much the same as the horse each aeroplane has individual characteristics, and the pilot like the equestrian must sense the particular qualities of the steed he is riding.

The Swift took the air like a thoroughbred, its well balanced controls so sensitive, they seemed to react immediately to one's thoughts by responding to the slightest touch and making the aircraft a joy to handle.

Quickly the Swift climbed above the smoke haze enshrouding the Manchester area, heading in a north easterly direction on what must have been close to the great circle course - the direct track - to Australia, a fact I did not realise until sometime later.

Nearly an hour sped by whilst I indulged in the delight of flying a perfect aeroplane, at the same time keeping constant check on my position in relation to the aerodrome.

With no map and not knowing the name of the aerodrome from which I had taken off, to lose myself and be forced to land to enquire my way, without being able to tell from whence I'd come, would not only be ridiculous, but would probably cause me a lot of trouble.

It was with reluctance I returned to earth, meeting with some difficulty in locating the aerodrome, because of the haze.

After expressing my thanks to Nic Comper, I asked the name of the aerodrome from which I'd flown. A query which brought forth a loud guffaw from Comper's colleague, who had thawed somewhat since my return. He announced that we were on Hooton aerodrome, that it was after four o'clock and time to do a little imbibing.

Concerned about the fleet passage of time, I declined an invitation to take 'a spot', and remounted my bicycle.

As I took my leave, Comper casually remarked. 'You ought to fly a Swift to Australia instead of joining Saunders-Roe'.

'And when would you like me to start, tomorrow?' I asked facetiously, as I rode away.

Back on the main road I realised it would be almost impossible for me to reach Birkenhead and locate my uncle's office before it closed, so I headed for Higher Bebbington, intending to go into Birkenhead with my uncle, the following day and make arrangements for returning to Australia.

Comper's jesting comment was a strange coincidence. Had he been serious and the Swift capable of making the flight, I may have disclosed my intention of returning to my homeland.

For a flight to Australia the fuel capacity would have to be increased to thrice its present capacity which would mean doubling the disposable load the Swift had been designed to carry and increasing the all up weight of the aircraft to more than twice its tare weight. A load of at least 300 lbs more than its authorised maximum take off weight.

Even if it were possible to fit a tank holding sufficient fuel and the Civil Aviation Authorities approved of the Swift being flown with this overload, a considerable amount of redesigning would be necessary, a job likely to take several weeks.

The idea of flying to Australia was great. With a suitable aeroplane it should be possible to get there in a week, but there was no sense in 'crying for the moon'.

At dinner that night I ate all that was placed before me much to the delight of my aunt, who monopolised the conversation, extolling the virtues of good food, plenty of exercise and regular habits. Such was my aunt's garrulity, I had no opportunity to tell of my adventures during the day.

Whilst we were having breakfast next morning, the mail arrived including a letter from Nic Camper requesting me to meet him at the Comper factory as soon as possible.

Asking my uncle if he would mind my paying him a visit at his office after I had seen Comper, I borrowed his bicycle and set out for Hooton immediately. On the way my imagination ran riot. Finally assuming Comper intended to offer me a job of test pilot.

After the previous day's flight Comper said he had been impressed by the way I had handled the Swift. He had also mentioned he was busy designing a new type, besides test flying the current production of Swifts.

An engineer who could fly and also knew a little about design might be very useful to a small company with great potential.

However, Mr Broadsmith would have to be consulted. It was possible he had offered me the draughtsman's job because of our past association, it was certainly not on account of my ability in a drawing office. His advice concerning my future would undoubtedly be wise. Nevertheless, wherever my future career lay, it was vital for me to return to Australia first.

I was soon to learn, however, that my conjecture was sadly astray. When I entered his office, Nic Comper, without preamble, said in his casual manner. 'About this flight with a Swift to Australia. It would be advisable to leave before the end of the month. Fogs can be very sticky in this part of the world in November, also from then on you could run into bad weather in the tropics, so we will get you away as quickly as we can.'

Too surprised to comment immediately, I stared at Comper wondering if he had taken leave of his senses. It was obvious the Swift with a still air range of less than 400 miles would be unsuitable for such a flight. Yet Comper was talking about a flight to Australia in less than three weeks.

As if reading my thoughts, Comper said, 'I have considered the range factor. It will be possible to produce a modified Swift capable of lifting enough fuel for a still air range of 900 miles with a margin of 5 gallons for emergencies. This will be sufficient to carry you over the Timor Sea, except against a headwind exceeding 40 knots. If such occurs you will have to delay the flight until the wind moderates'.

Still rather dazed I asked. 'When do you expect the aircraft to be ready?'

'Within twelve days, if there are no unforeseen snags and the A.R.B. expedite approval of the modifications. At the latest you should be able to leave on the 24th or 25th. It will be your responsibility to arrange for fuel, maps and other documents necessary for the trip.

'By the way', Comper continued, 'it would be wise for you to become as familiar as possible with the Swift, so take my machine up whenever it is available, but the first thing we have to do is take some measurements, with you in the cockpit.'

In the workshop a team of men had already commenced the conversion of a Swift under construction. For nearly an hour I sat in its fuselage skeleton whilst several draughtsmen took precise measurements of the meagre space between me and where the engine bulkhead would be. The only place an extra fuel tank could be fitted.

By reducing leg room to a minimum and moving the instrument panel back to within a few inches of my face, it was found that a tank with a capacity of approximately 25 gallons could be installed, bringing the total fuel capacity of the Swift to 41 gallons. This was 2 gallons less than Camper had estimated, but sufficient for covering the longest stage.

Although Comper had yet to obtain approval of his Board for the flight to Australia, he expected this to be a mere formality. He had, he said, called a special board meeting which would be held that afternoon. He expected the meeting to end about 5 o'clock, when he wanted me to meet his fellow directors. This reminded me that I had planned to leave Chester by train for Birmingham about 5p.m.

I explained my previous arrangements to Nic Comper, pointing out my aunts would be very upset when I failed to arrive.

'Send them a telegram', Comper advised, then 'No! I have a better idea. Fly my Swift down to Castle Bromwich (an aerodrome near Birmingham) and see your aunts, it may be your only chance before you leave for Australia, but be back by 5 o'clock without fail!

It was after 11 o'clock when Nic Comper and I walked on to the tarmac, where the trim red Swift was awaiting me. As I was about to board the aircraft, Comper's chairman - a large, dour looking man - Dawson by name arrived.

Comper mentioned the proposed flight to Australia and introduced me. The chairman peered at me then whined to Comper and said. 'That man doesn't appear to me to be the right type for flying one of our aircraft to Australia.'

Before I could utter a suitable retort, Comper - ignoring his chairman - said to me in his calm and quiet way. 'You had better make a start for Castle Bromwich, otherwise you will have little time at your disposal in Birmingham.'

I got into the Swift seething with indignation. Not that I objected to the chairman's opinion so much as to the way it had been expressed.

It was not the first time I had been humiliated in this manner. An incident which occurred at Narromine came to mind. There a woman who was about to take a joy flight, refused to fly when she discovered that I and not my engineer was the pilot. There had also been other instances when I had suffered similar embarrassment.

At one time I attempted to grow a beard, hoping this would give me an appearance more in keeping with my profession. After four days my image became so repulsive to me, I rid myself of the excresence.

Fortunately, by the time I had taxied the Swift to the take off position my anger had disappeared.

Those who venture aloft are likely to encounter a hazardous situation at any time from the starting of the engine, until it is silenced at the end of a flight. A potential which requires the constant and careful attention of the pilot who must be prepared to cope with any problem immediately.

Unaware I was to be faced with such a situation within the next few minutes, I took off, heading the Swift in the direction of Castle Bromwich.

A heavy haze hung in the atmosphere in the vicinity of Hooton, but visibility was much better to the south, not that I worried about finding my way. With the map - scale; 4 miles to 1 inch - Nic Comper had loaned me, it would be impossible to become lost except in zero visibility.

Yesterday I had been too busy getting the feel of the Swift and making sure I didn't lose myself to take particular notice of the terrain. Today I was able to pay more attention to the country slipping by noting places suitable for landing in the event of trouble.

Soon after takeoff the Swift was over hilly country, with small fields bounded by hedges and interspersed with thickets, rather like patchwork quilt in appearance. Beautiful to behold but quite unsuitable for a forced landing. It occurred to me how delightful it would be to drift above this lovely landscape in a balloon without the brain battering noise of an engine disturbing the peace.

As if in accord with this thought the noise of the engine suddenly ceased, so did my admiration for the country below, which I now viewed with extreme distaste.

Anxiously, I searched for a spot on which to land, but every field in sight seemed far too small to use without damaging the Swift. The meandering hedge lined lanes were also useless for this purpose.

I worked the throttle lever back and forth in the desperate hope the engine would come alive and pull the Swift out of its hazardous position, but there was no response.

With its propeller idly windmilling, the Swift lost height rapidly, a little red devil bent on its own and perhaps my destruction.

The field on which I finally decided to attempt a landing was very small, far too small, in fact, for my peace of mind, but it had the advantage of being on the side of a hill, also the hedge at the top end had plenty of foliage which I hoped would cushion the Swift at the end of its landing run without doing too much damage to the aircraft.

Although a considerable amount of concentration was required during the few remaining seconds before the inevitable happened, thoughts intruded about the impact this unhappy event would have on the Comper people. Even if the Swift escaped serious damage, it would have to be dismantled and transported back to the works by road.

Comper, himself, would properly appreciate the incident, but I visualized his chairman taking a poor view of the matter. It looked as if I would be travelling back to Australia by ship after all.

The ground came up quickly. Overshooting slightly, I sideslipped the Swift the last 100 feet, flattening out about 10 feet above the hedge at the bottom of the field.

Levelling out, it seemed as if the Swift was diving into the ground, the slope was much steeper than it seemed from the air, causing me to instinctively yank the 'stick' hard back forcing the nose up.

The Swift stalled, as none too gently the wheels contacted the ground and decelerated so rapidly it was obvious the aircraft would not only stop before reaching the hedge ahead, but would start rolling backwards down the slope as soon as it lost headway.

Alarmed at the possibility of the tail skid being broken and the rear of the fuselage damaged I kicked on hard left rudder swinging the Swift sideways across the slope where it came to rest about 80 feet from where it first alighted. By the grace of God Nic Comper's pride and joy had escaped damage.

Thankful, I sat in the cockpit waiting for my heart to climb down from my gullet and my knees to stop shaking. The field in which the landing had been made was about 250 feet square, well coated with grass and surrounded by high hedges beyond which little could be seen apart from the hills in the distance across the valley to the east and the roof of a farmhouse projecting above the hedge at the lower end of the ground.

Successfully bringing off a forced landing is always a boost to the ego, but in this instance my satisfaction was tempered by the knowledge that the Swift had to be removed from this restricted space.

The wiser course would be to dismantle the aircraft and take it back to Hooton by road, in fact, had the ground been level this would have been the only solution, because under normal circumstances it would be impossible for the Swift, despite its short take off characteristics, to clear the surrounding obstructions. However the slope was so steep, it might be just possible to fly the aircraft out by taking off downhill.

My contemplation of this matter was interrupted by a fox which warily approached, circled the Swift and then squatted down about 20 feet away.

Jumping out of the cockpit, I walked towards the animal which retreated a few yards, squatting down again when I paused remembering there were more important things to be done than chase a fox.

Turning, I made off down the hill towards a gate in the bottom corner of the field. I had gone only a few yards, when a man came through the gate and ran towards me.

Panting, he asked if I were alright. When I said 'Yes', he seemed surprised and enquired if the machine were broken. Ignoring my enquiry about the whereabouts of a telephone, he insisted on examining the Swift (the first aircraft he bad seen on the ground) before escorting me to the farmhouse, where, a few minutes later, I was able to contact the Comper works manager who despatched an engineer to investigate and if possible repair the engine.

Picton, the place where I had been forced down was very like Picton in NSW, although the country was more picturesque with hedgerows instead of fences and colourful trees instead of the gums abounding in the Picton NSW area.

Waiting for the engineer to arrive, I walked over the field examining the surface and still debating whether it would be possible to take the Swift off. The distance from hedge to hedge downhill, was 13 paces, sufficient under the existing circumstances, for the Swift to become airborne, taking off downhill. Whether the aircraft would clear the 15' hedge, was another matter. Fortunately the wind, very slight and blowing across the slope at not more than two or three miles per hour, was no hazard, although any change during the takeoff could be awkward.

Under normal circumstances, I would not have considered an attempt to fly away from this place, however I felt that if the Swift was taken back to Hooton by road, my chances of making the flight to Australia were very slim.

It was obvious the chairman of Comper's, who had already expressed his opinion of me, would be unlikely to alter his mind when he learned I had put down in a ground I was unable to fly the Swift away from.

The fox still squatting like a graven image, ignored me when I passed within a few feet of it, so I made a sudden move in its direction. Instead of running away, it moved in an almost leisurely fashion to the other side of the aircraft, still intently eyeing the machine.

I wondered what the animal was thinking. Was it trying to figure out what this strange object which had invaded its domain? Presently the engineer arrived accompanied by the farmer. Pointing to the fox I enquired if it were tame.

'He's not tame, he's curious. If I had a gun or dog, he'd be gone' the farmer replied.

We discovered the cause of the trouble was a petrol blockage, which was soon remedied.

Taxiing the Swift to the downwind corner at the top of the field and then pulling the tail as close to the hedge as possible, I got back into the cockpit feeling rather apprehensive. The hedge at the lower end of the ground appeared very close and the farmyard beyond, most of which was visible from this height, quite uninviting, particularly the pig sty.

As soon as the throttle was opened, the Swift charged down the hill, its nose so far below level flying position it gave the impression it was about to nose over. A few seconds of agonizing apprehension then the Swift took the air, skimming the hedge with inches to spare, and away upward to a safe altitude.

It is strange that, when suffering an experience of acute mental stress, some irrelevant incident makes the most vivid impression on the mind. In this instance, the fox, despite my efforts to dismiss the creature from my mind, occupied my thoughts most of the way to Castle Bromwich, where the Swift touched down 45 minutes after leaving Picton. Arriving more than 2 hours later than I had first anticipated.

With so little time remaining, my trip would have been in vain but for Captain Sutcliffe, the local aero club instructor, who persuaded one of his pupils to drive me to Handsworth, a Birmingham suburb, where my aunts conducted a private school.

My premature arrival didn't worry my aunts, in fact, they were rather pleased until I explained I could not stay and the reason why, they then became rather upset and confused. The old dears seemed unable to understand what I was talking about.

Having no time to go into details, I kissed them both goodbye, said I would write later, then rushed out to the car, which returned to Castle

Bromwich in record time. A few minutes later I was in the air again heading for Hooton, where, aided by a tailwind I made the 'deadline' with less than two minutes to spare.

Nic Comper came to meet me as I taxied the Swift on to the tarmac. Looking very pleased, he said his fellow directors had not waited for me because of the uncertainty of my arrival.

The engineer who had rectified the trouble at Picton, had reported the time I had taken off and there was some doubt about my being able to return to Hooton before dark.

A colourful account, by the engineer, of the Picton incident had been relayed to the board members by Comper, whose proposal concerning the Australian flight had, prior to this, received cool reception.

News of the successful forced landing had, however, resulted in a unanimous decision to proceed with the Australian flight.

Rather tired and slightly dazed by the day's events, I arrived back at Higher Bebbington shortly before 7 o'clock, realising my uncle and aunt must be concerned about my whereabouts. I had been expected back at lunchtime and by now should have been well on my way to Birmingham, by train.

It had been my intention to send a telegram to my uncle on my arrival at Birmingham, but the forced landing and the consequent delay caused me to forget to do so.

Entering the house with an apology on my lips, I was met by my uncle waving a form indignantly demanding. 'Please explain this'.

It was a telegram from one of my aunts. 'We think Arthur may be noncompos. He rushed here this afternoon saying he is flying to Australia. Can you enlighten us. Love Eleanor.'

Before I could speak my uncle continued. 'What do you mean by going to Birmingham this afternoon and upsetting your aunts by spinning some cock and bull story about flying off to Australia, then returning here at this time of night as if nothing had happened?'

'Until the telegram arrived your aunt and I were very worried, thinking you had met with an accident. If this is your idea of a joke it is a very poor one and hardly the behaviour of a sane man. You have some explaining to do, young man!' my uncle concluded heatedly.

My uncle, a meek quiet man, surprised me so much with his tirade I became so embarrassed and confused that I didn't know how to begin an explanation. My stuttered apology for forgetting to send a telegram added fuel to my uncle's wrath. 'Go on', he demanded, as I hesitated, finding it difficult to describe in a lucid manner all the events which had been crammed into my life since the previous day.

Starting from the time I had first seen an aircraft flying overhead, I related all that had happened to me up to the time of my return.

It was soon obvious my listeners believed me to be romancing, indeed, I could hardly believe the story myself, it all seemed like a marvellous dream.

When I had finished speaking my uncle and aunt continued to gaze at me in silence, which was broken, after what seemed ages, by a terse question from my uncle. Do you mean to tell us, a man you had just met was actually rash enough to invite you, a complete stranger, to fly his aeroplane, afterwards suggesting you fly it all the way to Australia?'

'Not satisfied with that fairy tale, you then embellish your story by saying the fellow loaned you the aeroplane so that you could go to Birmingham to see your aunts and upset them with this far-fetched tale. Even this is not enough. You add insult to injury by telling us you were compelled to land, on the way, in some outlandish place, where you were entertained by a fox.'

'Well it won't do my boy. It won't do!'

'We may be old English fogies, but we are not daft enough to swallow your tall colonial tales, which are fantastic enough to make Baron Munchausen turn in his grave.'

'You will apologise to your aunt and promise never to do such a thing again.'

During the silence which followed I tried to think of a way to clarify the present situation. My uncle's admonition aroused my anger, but I realised I was to blame and this was not the time for recrimination. The silence was broken by my aunt bursting into tears which aroused my uncle's anger again. There was nothing I could do to repair the situation so I made myself scarce. Had I not been so contrite, I would have fled the house, instead I went to bed, dog tired as much from emotional stress as anything.

With the intention of avoiding my uncle and his wife until such time as I could prove the veracity of my story, I slipped out of their house at dawn next morning to walk the 6 miles to Hooton.

Arriving shortly before 8 o'clock I was surprised to find Nic Comper already on the job, ironing out a snag on the airframe modification.

With him was George Edye, one of his directors. When they learned of the trouble with my relatives and of their disbelief of my story, George Edye kindly offered to take me back to Higher Bebbington and confirm the fact that I was flying to Australia.

Despite the unpleasant exercise of the previous night, my uncle and aunt seemed pleased when Edye deposited me at their door. His confirmation of my story started my aunt off with a fit of the vapours and caused my uncle to remark. 'I don't know what the world is coming to, the way young people carry on today. Rushing here and rushing there and doing incomprehensible things without a moments thought or consideration. When you arrived on Thursday night you said you were taking a job with Saunders-Roe and now you say you are going back to Australia and flying there into the bargain. A madcap idea if ever there was one. I don't understand it at all.'

My aunt, having dried her eyes, interrupted to ask me if I had had breakfast A question which reminded me, I had eaten nothing since the previous morning.

Both Edye and I were anxious to return to Hooton. but my aunt insisted on giving us tea and fruit cake before we left.

As we were leaving Edye told my uncle that I would be staying with him (the first I had heard of this arrangement) until my departure for Australia. I was too surprised to protest at the time, but did so on the way to the works. In reply Edye pointed out Higher Bebbington was rather remote and with no telephone at my uncle's home, to stay there was out of the question. 'Also by staying with me you will be under no obligation to anyone', he said.

'There will be no worry about informing anyone where you are going or what you are doing. You will be able to devote all your thought and energy to pursuing your preparation for the flight. My domestic staff will be at your disposal. My chauffeur will drive you anywhere at any time and should you require my help in any matter, you have only to ask', Edye concluded.

Although as enthusiastic about aviation as Nic Comper whom be greatly admired, George Edye, in all else was entirely different. A wealthy ex-army officer holding a substantial financial stake in the Comper company, George Edye knew little or nothing about the technical side of the aviation industry, nevertheless he seemed bent on spending most of his leisure time watching the new Swift take shape.

Immediately after returning to Hooton, I commenced planning my itinerary. I would have liked to have flown a great circle course to Australia, shorter by more than 1,000 miles, than the more conventional route via India, but Comper was not keen about the idea. He said that even if the Russians agreed to a flight over their territory, and that would be doubtful, nothing was known in England about facilities for flying in Siberia and Mongolia, nor about the weather or the attitude of the people in the remote parts it would be necessary to traverse.

The route via Austria and Turkey was also rejected because of the uncertainty of the weather at this time of year. This meant taking the longer route via France, Italy and Greece, over which there was less chance of encountering adverse weather.

Apart from determining the route to be flown and the countries for which permits and visas might be required, nothing more could be done until accurate maps, details of landing grounds and availability of fuel supplies had been obtained. A task that would have to be deferred until I visited London.

This was not the only delay, Nic Comper was also having difficulty with the redesign of the fuel system.

Because of the restricted space in the small cockpit it was quite a problem to position a manually operated fuel pump within handy reach without it being an obstruction to the pilot.

The matter was eventually resolved by making a small modification to the fuselage, enabling a semi-rotary hand pump to be installed in a position where it was possible to operate it without undue inconvenience. The auxiliary fuel tank was not linked directly with the engine. The fuel being delivered by way of the main tank.

About 1 o'clock, Nic Comper who had been working hard since dawn, suggested we adjourn to a nearby inn for lunch. Although the meal was mediocre, I fortified myself to such an extent that Nic Comper, unaware I had eaten nothing substantial since the previous morning, facetiously remarked, that I would have to moderate my intake, otherwise when the time came to leave for Australia, the cockpit of the Swift would be too small to accommodate me.

'So it was my light weight (125 lbs) which impelled you to invite me to take a Swift to Australia?' I quipped in return.

George Edye looked at Comper and said. 'I am 100% behind this project, but what puzzles me is why you suddenly decided to invite Butler to fly a Swift to Australia. Prior to yesterday you had never mentioned the idea'.

Comper thought for a while then said, 'The idea suddenly occurred to me while Butler was flying the Swift, last Friday. Come to think of it, I don't really know why I invited him to fly my machine. Subconscious intuition, I suppose. His description of Australian conditions certainly gave me the impression the Swift would be ideal for operations in that country. It is cheap to run and can be landed almost anywhere. There are many uses to which the aircraft can be put, and what better way of proving the Swift's worth than by flying one to Australia?

George Edye lived on the outskirts of Bromborough, only a few minutes drive from Hooton. Compared with my uncle's modest dwelling, Edye's home was rather pretentious. The bedroom I was to occupy was large enough to house a Swift and the adjoining bathroom so magnificent, my conception of the bathing habits of the English, gleaned from stories I had heard or read about the English way of life, was shattered.

Such opulence brought vivid memories of Gurley in northern New South Wales, where a bore trough, in an open paddock, served as a community bath for the villagers, who had unique rostering arrangements for taking their ablutions which, of course, could only be carried out at night.

Fresh from the experience of wallowing in a large glass enclosed bath, tussling with an elusive chromium serpent, which squirted a stream of scalding water when I inadvertently turned on a tap with my toe, and being nearly drowned by an icy flood ejected from a series of jets at the sides of the bath, I went in search of my host, eventually finding him warming his buttocks in front of a large coal fire which seemed rather out of place in this house of ultra modern plumbing.

Then I had the pleasure of being introduced to my hostess. Very reserved, tall, fair and beautiful, she was coincidently a namesake of the lady I loved.

Intending to leave for London at dawn, next morning, I retired early, but sleep eluded me. My mind was too active reviewing the events occurring during the past three days.

My decision to return to Australia seemed to have set off a sequence of events leading to my being given the opportunity of achieving my desire much quicker than I would have hitherto thought possible.

Although there was nothing unusual, under the circumstances, in my having impulsively entered that lane with the intention of making for Birkenhead to obtain information and if possible arrange transport to Australia by the fastest means, or even tarrying to idly watch an aeroplane landing. My subsequent action in returning to the aerodrome was as inexplicable as my taking a train to Liverpool instead of Weybridge. Then Nic Comper inviting me to fly his aircraft, followed by his casual suggestion that I should take a Swift to Australia might well be placed in the same category.

The rapidity with which a start had been made to produce an aircraft for this particular assignment and the acquiescence of Comper's fellow directors in this matter had created a situation which seemed to me to be fantastic.

It was as if some mysterious force - Providence if you will - was taking charge of my affairs, influencing hard headed business men to interrupt their normal tenor to enable me to achieve my heart's desire.

Even the chairman had been influenced against his prior judgement. A judgement which was not far wrong, for I was no reveller in audacious aeronautical adventure, in fact I was rather a timid type who treated flying with the utmost caution, and in normal circumstances, would have given no more consideration to a flight to Australia than one to the Moon.

The hazards likely to be encountered on such a flight were legion. An aggregate of over 2,500 miles of sea, a greater distance than that across the Atlantic between Liverpool and Halifax, had to be traversed. Nearly 24 hours flying during which should the engine fail, anywhere beyond gliding distance to the coast, I would most likely suffer the fate of Icarus.

Engine failure was not the only hazard. The range of the Swift even with the additional tank was comparatively short. Running into adverse weather could, quite easily, result in the Swift being forced down in some remote spot short of its objective, leaving me a prey for tigers, snakes and maybe crocodiles.

I envisaged the possibility of the compass failing at a time when it was vitally needed and other likely tribulations.

The more I dwelt on the matter the more foolhardy this flight seemed, nevertheless, although the idea appalled me I was determined this would be one instance of a faint heart winning a fair lady.

My fears and foreboding had vanished next morning when I jumped out of bed at 5 o'clock.

George Edye's chauffeur drove me to the aerodrome and soon afterwards I was aloft, bound for London via Cowes, where I intended to explain to Mr Broadsmith my reason for returning to Australia and ask him to allow me to join Saunders-Roe early in the new year, when I expected to return to England with a wife.

Although the English countryside may not be the most beautiful in the world, the hills and dales of Cheshire, Salop and Worcestershire, dressed in various shades of green, splashed with crimson and gold, all contrasting in a perfect harmony of colour, delicately changing as the Sun came up through the haze in the south east, was a glorious sight on the cold, calm and clear autumn morning. Even the towns, enroute, with their roads and railways radiating out like spiders legs, failed to mar the scene.

The Severn Valley between Bridgenorth and Stourport with the Wyre Forest spread out in all its leafy grandeur was one of the finest sights I had ever seen.

26

Viewing scenes such as this was one of the things which made flying so attractive. A privilege denied earthbound creatures.

The lovely vale of Evesham fringed by the Cotswold Hills, and entrancing to the eye, slid by beneath. Ahead lay Swindon and just beyond a heavy veil of fog lay athwart my track, obscuring the landscape as far as the eye could see.

Hoping the Isle of Wight would be in the clear I continued on over the dazzling sheet of white stratus stretched out below, smooth as a well ironed tablecloth. Half an hour later, with no sign of a break in the fog I turned back, realising the Swift must be well out over the English Channel and that the only way I might reach my destination was by returning to the northern extremity of the fog hoping that it may have lifted sufficiently to allow enough space to fly beneath.

The sense of speed thrills most people and hazardous though it maybe, flying near the surface across open country or over a surf fringed beach has an irresistible fascination which few airman can resist.

Seeing an opportunity of enjoying the thrill of 'skimming' without danger of running into a stray telegraph line or voracious seagull, I dropped the Swift until its wheels were brushing the white mass. Suddenly the aircraft shot over a hole in the fog giving me a fleeting glimpse of a railway line some 2000 feet below.

A quick turn and the Swift was in a steep spiral going down a funnel so small I frequently lost sight of the ground. 50 or 60 ft above the surface, horizontal visibility extended for about 500 to 600 yards.

Anticipating the fog to be in the process of dispersing, I followed the railway, leading to the south east. Within a few minutes the Swift was over docks and I was kept busy dodging a number of masts reaching up into the overcast. Becoming more alarmed every second, I was about to climb the Swift up through the fog when visibility improved to half a mile or more ahead, showing clear water rippled by a slight breeze. Then the fog closed in once more, but a second or so later visibility improved again, giving the impression the fog was dispersing.

Disinclined to climb through the overcast and abandon the attempt to reach Cowes which might be in the clear and by my reckoning not more than 12 miles away, I continued on course above the water, which I guessed to be Southampton Water.

A few seconds later the Swift entered another blanket of fog so dark it must have contained a considerable amount of smoke. Then the Swift was in the clear again and right in its path a large liner with red funnels, so close I was forced to zoom the Swift upwards vertically. So narrow was the margin, the wheels of the aircraft seemed to be rolling up the side of one of the funnels which suddenly disappeared as the Swift entered the fog, almost stalling before I was able to get the nose down to gather speed before climbing out of a very frightening situation.

The Swift dropped out of the overcast before enough speed had built up to start climbing. Open country had replaced the water, with visibility extending for a hazy half mile.

The near collision with the ship had given the nerves of my stomach, already suffering the pangs of hunger, a nasty jolt, and making me fully aware there was no future in this sort of flying, but with Cowes less than 6 minutes flight away and visibility apparently improving, I decided to go on, dropping the Swift down to about 20 feet above the ground.

Ahead the flat meadows enclosed by low hedges stretched away for nearly a mile before merging with the haze.

Anticipating the Swift would reach the Solent, the stretch of water separating the Isle of Wight from the mainland within the next 2 minutes and be over Cowes in another three, my spirits began to rise. Suddenly the overcast seemed to drop out of the sky, instantly blotting out the view ahead.

Quickly closing the throttle I felt for the ground. The wheels touched and the Swift sped through the murk. Switching off the ignition I prayed fervently for the aircraft to stop before colliding with the hedge which had, a few seconds ago, been visible about 500 yards ahead.

Most aeroplanes are easy to maneuvre once they are airborne, but on the ground control of an aircraft is very restricted, particularly after landing. Having no wheel brakes, the friction of the tail skid dragging along the ground is the only means of slowing down.

Although the tail skid on some aircraft is linked with the rudder control so that the aircraft can be turned on the ground, change of direction can only be made slowly, otherwise the aircraft would go over onto its wing tip, or even worse flip on to its back.

Feeling helpless and sweating profusely as the Swift trundled through the murk towards the unseen hedge, I realised I bad been rather foolish in persisting in the attempt to reach Cowes.

After what seemed ages, the Swift slowed to a stop in fog so thick the wing tips were barely visible.

The type of fog I had hitherto experienced, in Australia, formed on the ground during the night or early hours of the morning, sometimes enshrouding the landscape for several hours after sunrise, but when the fog started to rise and disperse, the improvement would be progressive. Here the conditions seemed to be the reverse. The catabatic behaviour of the fog now enshrouding me was a menace which had taught me a lesson I would long remember.

It also brought to mind the advice of an old pilot of bygone days. Frank by name and frank by nature, be was always asserting. 'Never trust wine, women or the weather. Given the chance they sour your belly, sadden your heart and soften your brain'.

Jumping from the cockpit, half frozen, I stamped around the Swift to get my blood circulating again. The fog felt as if it was penetrating to my bones, soon forcing me to return to the partial protection of the cockpit where I debated whether to stay in the Swift until the fog lifted or go in search of something to eat.

I listened intently for sounds which might indicate the direction of some habitation, with the exception of the noise of moisture dripping from the woods not a sound could be heard now that the contraction noises of the engine had ceased.

Sitting still, slowly freezing whilst the pangs of hunger made ever increasing demands to be satisfied became almost unbearable. A state of affairs which spurred me to action.

Perusing the map and mentally tracing my course since passing over the docks, which I assumed to be in the vicinity of Southampton, I guessed the landing had been made somewhere south of Netley. Taking a bearing from the compass, I set out northward in the direction of where Netley might be.

Walking slowly and trying to keep a straight course, an almost impossible task when you can't see where you are going, I paused frequently to listen for the sound of traffic or any sound for that matter which would reassure me I was still in the land of the living.

The enshrouding blanket of clammy fog and the uncanny silence created a sense of unreality. I might well have been one of H.G. Wells' characters and the Swift a time machine which had projected me into a past age or a future era.

A feeling of claustrophobia brought the desire for something to break the silence. There was nothing to prevent me from singing, whistling or even talking to myself, except by so doing I might fail to hear some sound which could lead me out of this moist purgatory.

Some 15 minutes passed without a sound being heard and nothing seen except a few feet of grass and the encircling fog. It was obvious I was lost and weaving a crooked course, otherwise the boundary of the field would have been reached long before this.

Too late I realised it would have been wiser to have started off towards the hedge - which could not have been more than a few feet away from the nose of the Swift - then to have followed the boundary until reaching a gate or a track which might have lead to more civilised parts.

I stood and considered what I should do, then motivated by cold I started to run, but only for a few feet. The thought of falling into a quarry or colliding with some obstacle caused me to proceed more cautiously, which was wise, because almost immediately, I nearly collided with a wall so high the top was hidden by the fog. Quite elated by this sign of civilization, I carefully made my way along the wall, which ended suddenly after I had taken less than half a dozen steps.

Unaware of the surprise in store within the next few seconds, I hesitated, wondering whether I should retrace my steps. The noise of a car starting up somewhere ahead caused me to continue on. A few steps further and I was on a path along which I bumped into someone coming in the opposite direction. Someone I recognised.

'Wilfred Andrews' I shouted, 'How glad I am to see you.' Andrews, who was as surprised as I, wanted to know where I had come from and how I had arrived.

When I told him I had been forced down somewhere in the vicinity by the fog Andrews comments were far from complimentary.

'How did you find the aerodrome?', be questioned.

When I asked, 'What aerodrome?' Andrews seemed rather surprised and sceptical that I was unaware that I was on Hamble aerodrome. But how was I to know? The place wasn't marked on my map and no hangars could be seen.

Wilfred Andrews, a young engineer, was a fellow member of the staff of Australian Aerial Services at Hay, at the time I had rebuilt the old Avro 504K, the aircraft on which I had learned to fly.

Wilfred, who helped me rig the Avro, had shared a unique experience with me, an experience which might well have ended Wilfred's career.

It happened when Francis Briggs, who was teaching me to fly, was transferred to. Melbourne for several weeks, just as he had started my instruction, an irksome interruption which did not deter me from going out to the aerodrome each morning well before the time for starting work. Wilfred Andrews usually accompanied me and we would sit in the Avro discussing the art of flying.

One morning - perfect for taking the air - the urge to do something more than talk impelled me to start the engine and with Wilfred in the back seat, I taxied the Avro about the aerodrome completely forgetting the time.

The Avro was at the far side of the ground when I suddenly realised we should be at work. John Stubbs who was in charge at Hay was a good fellow, but he was a great stickler for punctuality and could be rather terse concerning any laxity in this respect. With this in mind I opened the engine to full throttle to cross the aerodrome as quickly as possible. The tail of the machine came up immediately and before I realised it, the Avro was off the ground which was receding further every second.

So far my flying experience had been confined to doing gentle turns at an altitude of 2,000 feet. Mastering the art of taking off and landing had yet to come, but I knew the theory of performing these maneuvres by reading Flight Commander McMinnes' book *Practical Flying*. The contents of which I almost knew by heart, particularly his description of landing. "In landing, a pupil first cuts off the engine, puts the machine at the correct gliding angle by moving the control lever forward".

"Assuming that he sees that he will hit off the landing ground correctly, he must watch the earth most intently, keeping up his correct gliding angle and speed all the while".

'When he gets to within 20 ft or 30 ft of the earth be can begin almost imperceptibly to flatten out by manipulating the control lever in just the same way as that in which he took the machine off the ground a few minutes before".

"Still watching the ground intently about 20 yards or 30 yards or even more in front of the machine, he continues to pull back the lever ever so gently until he gradually decreases his flying angle and finally as the machine loses its flying speed, its angle of descent is blended in the horizontal of the ground without the slightest jerk and the machine comes to earth".

"In easing back the control lever, it may be necessary at times to pause momentarily or even move the stick forward slightly if the backward movement has been made too suddenly or too much and has resulted in the machine being unduly held up, or even made to 'balloon'."

"The whole art of landing consists in accurately timing the relative position of the ground and the machine by the eye working in perfect unison with the hand".

Words easy to read and to remember, but not so easy to follow.

Cutting off the engine power, I glanced at the ground with no idea of its distance. It could have been anything from 8 to 18 feet or even more for all I knew.

Should I follow, the book by moving the control lever forward putting the machine into a glide or was the ground close enough to pull back the control lever - according to the words of the book - for the final stage?

Whilst debating the matter with myself, the Avro, deprived of its motive power, floated back to earth. Perhaps not in the manner which Commander McMinnes would have approved, but safely for all that.

As the Avro touched down, there was a jolt and the aircraft swung to the right. I managed to check the swing, the Avro eventually rolling to a stop a few feet from the hangar.

Turning round to comment to Wilfred about our adventure I was amazed to find he was no longer in the machine. He appeared out of the dust stirred up by the machine, a few seconds later, looking very dirty, in a frightful temper and rather abusive.

Andrews had become very alarmed when he realised the Avro had taken the air in my inexpert hands. Rather than risk being killed in the crash which he thought inevitable, he decided to leap from the aircraft.

Fortunately he jumped just as the Avro returned to earth. That he had escaped injury except for a few bruises, was remarkable considering the aircraft was travelling at least 35 miles per hour.

Wilfred Andrews was a good fellow who soon recovered his temper, but never his confidence in me as a pilot.

We lost touch when he left Hay shortly after this incident and I had often wondered what had become of him. Now nearly a decade later it was a very pleasant surprise to meet him again.

Andrews was now one of the instructors at the Air University at Hamble. The only one of its kind in the world, this university operated by Air Services Training, provided instruction in every phase of aviation from engineering to economics.

Run on lines similar to a military academy, it was commanded by Group Captain Barton, who when he learned of my plan to fly to Australia, suggested that I would be wise to take a course in navigation at the university.

When told I was due to leave within a few days, the Group Captain wished me luck, adding that I would need it. A point I was not prepared to argue.

Navigation is without doubt a precise science, but I failed to see how this science, as practised by the mariner, could be applied effectively by an aviator. Maybe in a future age, aircraft will be developed to the extent it will be possible to install and utilize, during flight, all the equipment necessary for accurate navigation.

At the present time even the best of navigators would find it impossible to apply their art with precision whilst piloting an aeroplane, because of the speed at which an aircraft travels, its three dimensional movement and other factors such as unreliable instruments, the fickleness of the wind and the restricted space to which a pilot is confined.

Careful preflight planning, vigilant observation and applied common sense in the air, aided by the grace of Providence are, in the main, the essentials for successful aerial journeying.

Approximately 2 hours after my arrival, the fog thinned sufficiently for the Hangars and buildings nearby to be seen, but another hour elapsed before the Swift was revealed in the far corner of the aerodrome within a few feet of the hedge fronting it.

The latest weather report revealed that Cowes was fogbound and likely to remain so. The 'London area was clear, but weather was deteriorating, with the possibility of fog blanketing the western suburbs within another hour. News which caused me to lose no time in taking off for Heston, a flight of about 35 minutes.

North and east visibility had improved to about 2 miles when the Swift climbed out of Hamble, it was too hazy, however, to see Southampton, also the cloud was clinging to the ground, in the south.

At 600 feet the wings of the Swift were scraping the cloud base. A few minutes later the rising surface of the Downs came up to join the clouds.

Mindful of my earlier experience, I immediately turned back towards Hamble. Soon, however, the cloud closed down, in every direction, right to the ground, forcing me to climb the Swift up through the overcast.

Flying in cloud is a most unpleasant experience, because without a visible horizon it is impossible to tell the exact altitude of the aircraft. In theory, flying an aeroplane by instruments should be possible without reference to the horizon. This can be done if the atmosphere is calm, however should there be any turbulence, it is not possible to control the aeroplane properly for any length of time, because the instruments are unable to effectively register the movement of the aircraft so that the pilot can make adjustments precisely and accurately enough to keep the aeroplane on even keel.

In addition to fallibility of the instruments, the pilot when flying in cloud is subjected to a phenomenon produced by his senses, giving him the impression the aeroplane is behaving in an abnormal manner when it is not.

Resisting the desire to obey the impulse giving this false impression requires the exertion of considerable will power, which if prolonged can be mentally exhausting.

By the time the Swift had thrust itself out of the top of the overcast, I was sweating at the palms from fighting against the desire to push the control stick forward to counteract the feeling that the aircraft was assuming an ever increasing climbing gradient which must surely end in a stall, although the air speed indicator was registering a steady 70 miles per hour.

A great change had taken place aloft since my early morning flight. The sun, which had previously caused such a dazzling reflection from the cloud below, was now obscured by a layer of high stratus which had drifted in, sandwiching the Swift in a haze which blotted out the horizon.

It looked as if the weather was deteriorating more rapidly than I had been led to expect, with the top layer of cloud closing down on that below and enshrouding the Swift in dark, dank Valuer.

With the cloud came slight turbulence and a renewed battle with my senses. Had the altimeter and airspeed indicator been less sluggish and the compass needle less inclined to gyrate, it might have been easier to ignore the mental prompting which I knew to be false. As it was the Swift, despite my efforts, seemed to be weaving its way like a tipsy traveller.

After an indeterminable time, the Swift sped out of the cloud into misty sunlight which made me feel much better despite the unbroken layer of cloud below.

Reckoning about 50 miles had so far been covered, I was now faced with having to descend through the overcast or carry on until a break appeared in the cloud. The idea of overshooting my destination - no more than 12 miles away if my reckoning was correct - to end up goodness knows where, was almost as unpalatable as going down through the cloud with the possibility of crashing into some obscured obstruction below.

Deciding on the lesser of two evils, hoping the weather would improve on the far side of the metropolis, I continued on course, putting the Swift into a climb to clear the London area at a reasonable altitude.

A minute or so later, I saw far to the south what appeared to be a break in the cloud. This disappeared before the Swift reached it. As I turned the Swift back to its original heading, a friendly zephyr parted the cloud revealing a narrow strip of clear country below. Back came the throttle, as I hurried the Swift earthward as quickly as possible.

The Swift was down to less than 2000 feet and losing height rapidly when the ground suddenly vanished.

Easing out of the dive, I continued the descent in a more cautious manner, hoping to break into the clear before being forced to take her up again. Down at 400 feet, no longer able to stand the strain of this blind descent, I opened up the engine and eased back the stick. As the nose started to lift, the Swift cleared the cloud about 250 feet above meadows which stretched away into the haze devoid of any recognisable landmark, not even a road being within the range of vision. A check of the course showed the Swift had swung about 40 degrees after the cloud closed in. It was now heading almost due north, I knew not where. Hoping some recognisable landmark would appear soon, I kept to the present heading for a couple of miles, when a railway showed up and soon after a town, where I took the Swift down over the railway station to read the name.

Woking. I then climbed back to just beneath cloud to check my position on the map. By the time this had been done the Swift was over Brooklands, the famous motor track enclosing the aerodrome where the first aeroplane to be flown to Australia, the Vicker's Vimy, was built.

The weather started to deteriorate again as the Swift approached the Thames, visibility closing in until it was no more than half a mile and gradually becoming worse.

Rather concerned about the possibility of hitting a large gasometer, which I had been told, was alongside the boundary of Heston aerodrome, I was about to turn back to land at Brooklands, when the hangars at Heston loomed up.

By the time the Swift was down and on the tarmac, visibility was no more than 100 yards and getting worse.

Although the flight from Hamble had taken less than three quarters of an hour, it had seemed much longer than that, particularly the period when the Swift was flying in cloud, which had been a very nerve wracking experience.

The necessity for me to fly in cloud had never arisen previously. Most times I had been able to get beneath or around. On the rare occasions when this had been impossible I had turned back, being fully aware of the dire results likely, in the event of an engine failure in conditions where the cloud base extended to. the ground.

However, the most disturbing feature was the strange feeling concerning the attitude of the aeroplane when flying in cloud. A sensation which made me doubt my ability to fly for any length of time under these conditions. That similar circumstances were most likely to occur, at some time or the other, on the flight between England and Australia, worried me considerably.

At Heston, a young aviatrix, who had been forced by the weather to abandon flying for the day, offered me a lift to London in her car. A charming English girl, who if she could fly as well as she could drive, might well vie with Amy Johnson as a pilot.

Proceeding towards the city the fog and the traffic thickened gradually until the car was forced to crawl in low gear, surrounded by vehicles dimly seen through, what the driver termed, 'a peasouper'. After a nightmare journey lasting over 2 hours, the car crawled out of the murk towards the eastern end of Piccadilly where an amber sun was trying to penetrate a sulphurous atmosphere.

During the many enforced stops enroute, the driver satisfied her curiosity about me, my country and its people. She also offered me some advice concerning my proposed flight, including a suggestion that I should obtain my maps and carnets from the Automobile Association, where she kindly dropped me.

My charming mentor had driven away before I realised I knew neither her name or address. I would have liked to have thanked her for her advice which proved to be very good.

Within half an hour the Automobile Association had agreed to supply maps and carnets, which were to be sent to Hooton as soon as they had been prepared.

Two days later all visas and flying permits had been obtained except those for Persia and arrangements made with the Vacuum Oil Company for fuel supplies along the route.

When I visited the Air Ministry to inform them of my projected flight, they decided to issue me with a British pilots licence because I would be flying an aircraft with British registration. I also obtained a red lined canvas cape to protect my neck from the sun and some food tablets, in case I was forced down in some spot where food was unobtainable. About the size of an aspirin each tablet was supposed to equal a normal meal, it was not very palatable, but a sample certainly filled me up, so much so, I was unable to eat any lunch afterwards.

The next day, 15th October, I planned to fly the Swift back to Hooton, calling in at Castle Bromwich to visit my aunts and try to persuade them that I was not as mad as they thought.

Unfortunately the weather which had been atrocious during my stay in London, was in my opinion too bad for flying, so I decided to leave the Swift at Heston and travel by train.

Shortly before I was due to leave I received a telephone call from a representative of Pollock-Brown, an organisation which had - so my caller claimed - produced a new type of instrument that would revolutionize flying.

Hearing about my proposed flight to Australia the Pollock-Brown man wanted to demonstrate this wonderful aid which would enable an aircraft to be flown safely in any kind of weather.

I declined the invitation saying I was about to leave for Birmingham.

'Splendid', said the Pollock-Brown man. 'We will fly you to Castle Bromwich'.

When I pointed out the weather was definitely unsafe for flying, I was told. 'Not for an aircraft fitted with a Pollock- Brown Deviator. With this instrument flying is as safe and as simple as walking down the street.'

The protest I started to make was ignored. The voice on the phone continued. 'No sensible aviator would consider flying in bad weather without this aid. I am sure a demonstration will convince you, I am therefore taking the liberty of calling for you within the next few minutes.'

Lacking the moral courage to refuse without an adequate excuse I was taken to Hanworth aerodrome, where I was given an excellent lunch which reminded me, like that of a man condemned to the scaffold, this meal would quite likely be my last.

My frame of mind was not improved by the glib talk of my host who well and truly fortified himself with liquid refreshment during lunch, after which be led me out through the pouring rain to a Dessouter monoplane.

Captain James, the pilot, seemed unconcerned about the inclement weather. In response to my comment, he remarked. 'All the better for demonstrating the Deviator'.

Although I was seated behind the pilot I had a clear view of the instruments, particularly the Deviator, the functioning of which was explained by Captain James.

Beside me on the bench seat the salesman kept up a commentary on the virtues of the Deviator and the advisability of fitting this aid in the aircraft I intended flying to Australia, until the noise of the engine starting drowned his voice.

The aircraft moved forward through the pelting rain which fell from the scudding clouds, no more than 300 feet above.

Cloud was reported down to ground level on the Chilton Hills which lay athwart our course with bad visibility at Castle Bromwich.

A forecast which caused us to feel very dejected as the machine swung round into wind for the takeoff and more despondent still when the wheels parted company with the sodden ground. I anxiously watched the earth disappear as the aircraft climbed into the cloud, and wondered if I would live to fly another day.

Despite the slight turbulence the instruments remained steady only the rotation of the second hand around the clock dial, the almost imperceptible movement of the altimeter needle showed. The disc of the Deviator, slightly above the cross grid, indicated a steady climb, and so far all seemed well.

The altimeter was touching the 5,000 feet mark when the pilot eased back the throttle and shouted, 'Watch this', as he pulled back the joy stick and kicked in left rudder, half rolling the aircraft into a spin.

After the first sensation of movement, there was no physical indication of the aircraft spinning earthward, although the rotating compass needle, the airspeed indicator flicking below the stall mark and the unwinding altimeter showed the machine was out of control. The P.B. Deviator disc was moving round inside its casing in a peculiar manner which didn't mean a thing to me.

Horrified by the action of the pilot who had placed us in such dire peril, I watched with ever increasing anxiety, the altimeter needle move down past the 3,000 feet mark, my stomach cringing; anticipating the crash into the cloud clothed hills below us, and the resulting holocaust which must surely occur in the next few minutes.

The altimeter registered 2,800 feet, then 2,700 feet. Unable to contain myself any longer, I shouted at the immobile pilot. 'Why the hell don't you do something?' he turned and said calmly. 'Keep your hat on'. The salesman then said something, but his remark was drowned by the noise of the engine being opened up. A glance at the instruments showed the airspeed indicating 70 miles per hour, the altimeter registering 2,500 feet with its pointer rising. The compass had stopped its giddy spin, its needle showing the aircraft to be on its original course. A miracle had happened.

That particular bit of the Chiltem countryside beneath us remained unspoiled and the patrons of the nearest village 'pub' had been deprived of a bit of gruesome gossip.

It didn't take long for the Dessouter to regain altitude. At 5,000 feet, the pilot again throttled the engine and shouted 'I will now show you a recovery from a right hand spin.'

Dismayed by this further tempting of Providence, I shouted, 'No!' I am quite satisfied the Deviator is all that you claim it to be. Just get me to Castle Bromwich as soon as possible. I will have a Deviator installed in the Swift if the Comper people will agree.'

The Dessouter freed itself from the clouds near Warwick and a few minutes later was touching down at Castle Bromwich.

Still rather shaken by my experience, I watched the Dessouter disappear into the haze on its return flight, feeling very thankful for being back on earth again, having had more than enough cloud flying. Although I was not unduly timid, I was not one of those fearless fellows who enjoyed having his hair raised and certainly disliked having my suprarenal glands, or whatever they are, over exercised, needlessly.

The engine of the Dessouter failed on the way back to London and the machine finished its journey stuck in a hedge instead of at Handworth. Fortunately neither the pilot nor the salesman was injured.

During my short stay in Birmingham, my aunts changed their opinion of me. I was no longer suspected of insanity, instead, in their eyes I had become a courageous adventurer. 'A modern Francis Drake' to quote my elder aunt.

I did not tell them of my craven feelings during the flight from London, it would have been such a pity to have disillusioned them.

On my return to Hooton, next day (16th October), Doctor Pobjoy invited me to help with the assembly of the engine which would power the Swift for the Australian flight.

The engine was completed and test run late on Monday, 19th October, and sent over immediately to the Comper works.

Doctor Pobjoy, who supervised the assembling of the engine personally, gave me a thorough grounding on its characteristics and the method of operation for getting the best out of the little beauty which weighed no more than 130 lbs.

During the time I had been away from the Comper works great progress had been made with the Swift. Only the installation of the engine and some painting required to be done before the aircraft was ready to fly.

The route maps arrived next morning, sixteen altogether, most of them different in size, projection and scale which varied from 1-1,000,000 to 1-5,000,000.

Although the maps had cost £32 - only six pounds less than my steamship fare from Australia - they were well worth the money. Each contained a wealth of detail, even the small scale 1-5,000,000 map which covered the whole of the Malay Peninsula.

I spent most of the day studying the maps and carefully marking the proposed route, with several alternates, in case of deviations. It was necessary for this preliminary work to be accurate, in fact it was as important as the actual flying.

When all the courses and distances had been marked down and checked, I spent an hour or so day dreaming, going over the route on a 'flight of fancy' which later proved to be sadly astray. Even my preconception of the aerodromes enroute, bore no resemblance to those on which I landed during the actual flight.

Planning to depart from Lympne, the nearest aerodrome to the Continent with customs facilities, at 30 minutes past midnight on the 25th October, five days hence, to arrive about 9am at Rome, which was just within range of the Swift, provided there was no headwind. Then after refuelling and breakfast, go on to Athens, where I anticipated landing as the shades of night were falling.

Departing from Athens early the following morning with the intention of arriving at Aleppo early in the afternoon of the same day and after checking the aircraft and engine, continue over Arabia during the cool night hours, getting to Basra, where I hoped to land by the light of the moon about midnight. Leaving here immediately after refuelling, to arrive in Jask just in time for breakfast and so to Karachi before nightfall.

At Karachi, I intended to rest for twelve hours, leaving here in time to get to Jhansi before dark and on to Calcutta by sunrise next morning.

Taking off from Calcutta as soon as possible, I hoped to arrive at Rangoon during the afternoon of the fifth day out from England and be at Singora by daybreak the following day.

The course on this section was more southerly than hitherto and with the long autumn nights behind me I should be able to reach Cheribon, in Java, on the sixth day, even after stopping at Singapore to refuel. Of course, a head wind could upset this schedule, but if this happened I would spend the night at Batavia. I had no intention of making any night landing after leaving Basra, because I expected to be rather fatigued towards the end of each day, as the flight progressed and unable to cope safely with landings after dark.

The following night I hoped to reach Kupang, leave here about midnight to arrive at Darwin early next morning. Then after clearing customs and breaking my fast, fly on to Camooweal, where I planned to have a good nights rest, before my final hop to Tooraweenah which I expected to reach during the afternoon of the 2nd of November. Nine days after leaving England.

Only 25 days would have elapsed since the receipt of the letter which had impelled me to make this journey. However the letter had been written 37 days prior to that, a total of 62 days.

Plenty of time for my rival to propose, but hardly sufficient to marry the young lady. There was also a chance of the fellow being tardy in 'popping the question', as well as the possibility of the young lady rejecting such a proposal. Nevertheless, I intended getting to Tooraweenah as fast as the Swift could carry me.

'I doubt if you will be able to adhere to this schedule', Nic Comper said, when he saw my itinerary. 'It would be a splendid effort to cut the record to Australia by more than two days, but I doubt if you or anyone else could do it in the time you have allotted, because you haven't allowed for adequate rest.'

'No one could be more delighted than I to see you break the record, but you are more likely to break your neck attempting to maintain such a pace.'

All we want you to do is get the Swift to Australia in one piece. To think of flying over 14 hours on the first day, followed by an attempt to fly for 27 hours without rest is absurd in my opinion'. Comper concluded.

'It isn't so absurd if you look at it from my point of view'. I retorted. 'The Swift is quite able to maintain this schedule in reasonable weather and with freedom of mechanical trouble. It is an easy machine to fly and I am physically fit.'

'Lindbergh was airborne for over 33 hours when he flew from New York to Paris and Miss Elinor Smith established an endurance record by staying aloft for nearly 27 hours. If a seventeen year old girl can remain in the air for that period I am sure I could.

The chief reason for planning such a tight schedule was to make sure there would be no delay on the ground should I be fortunate enough to have similar conditions to those Smithy experienced last year, when he flew the whole way from England to Australia in ideal weather.'

When I pointed this out, Comper said, 'Very well, have it your way'.

After sending details of the itinerary to the Vacuum Oil company my preflight arrangements were complete except for the Persian permit which I expected to receive that day.

When the permit failed to arrive by the afternoon post, Nic Comper, who anticipated the completion of the new Swift on the following day, 21st October, suggested I try to expedite matters by flying down to London in his aircraft, which one of his friends had flown back from Heston.

The weather next morning was a great contrast to that on the day of the flight from Hanworth. A perfect Indian Summer day with a pale blue sky unmarred by a single cloud. Conditions so perfect, that when I arrived over London shortly before 8 o'clock, instead of landing at Heston, I flew on to Lympne, intending to inspect the aerodrome from which I would make my departure.

Half an hour later the Swift was losing height over the coast of Kent, the Cinque Ports spread out below. Green hills and white cliffs bordered the English Channel glistening in the sunshine, stretching away to the coast of France clearly defined to the south east.

The landing at Lympne - a green sword on the edge of the Downs overlooking Romney Marsh - was a 'touch and go', because I was anxious to be at the Persian Consulate when it opened for business at 10 o'clock.

A head wind retarded the Swift on the way back to Heston, so I landed at Croydon, the aerodrome used by the international airways serving London 12 miles or so away to the north.

Arriving in the city a few minutes after ten, I was kept waiting for over an hour at the consulate. By then, my patience having reached the end of its endurance, I decided to go to Caxton House, the headquarters of the Vacuum Oil company in London, to see if a landing on Persian soil could be avoided by refuelling at some place on the Arabian coast of the Persian Gulf.

As I started for the entrance, a fellow came over requesting me to follow him. He escorted me to an office where, after careful scrutiny by a foreign gentleman, I was asked the reason for applying for a permit to fly over and landing in Persia.

When my explanation had been given, my passport was demanded by the interrogator. After careful perusal, a page was selected to which their highly ornate stamps were affixed and franked with the consulate seal. Then after what seemed an after thought the official produced a large rubber stamp the imprint of which covered the remainder of the page. Over this he scrawled some hieroglyphics which I assumed would entitle me to wing my way across Persia and land in that country without hindrance.

The scribe finally finished his task and after I had paid the fee demanded, my passport was handed back by the official who then informed me that in due course I would be informed whether or not permission to fly over Persia would be granted.

With a feeling of frustration I asked why my passport had been endorsed with the permission to land in their country. In reply the official told me that I had received a visa which all travellers to Persia must possess before entering their country.

'Taking an aeroplane there is another matter. Permission to do this requires further consideration, the official said.

Unmoved by my plea for a permit to be issued forthwith, the Persian replied, 'it is a matter for Teheran to decide, they will do so in due course.'

Upset by this unsatisfactory state of affairs I hurried over to Caxton House where I learned that, although there were no aerodromes, it might be possible to land on Bahrain Island or at Maskat, however there was no fuel available at either of these isolated spots, and it would take at least three weeks to deliver supplies which would have to be shipped by Dhow from either Karachi or Basra.

Rather disheartened by this news I returned to Hooton just in time to see Nic Cornper test the new Swift. It seemed almost unbelievable that so much had occurred since Comper and I had first met 12 days ago.

After the first test flight, Doctor Pobjoy, Nic Comper and two or three more of us concerned with the project, adjourned to the clubhouse to celebrate. Here we were joined by two well known personalities. The Master of Sempill - who later flew a Puss Moth to Australia - and John Walker who had flown in from Scotland on his way to London. Even this convivial company failed to dispel my sour mood.

Nic Comper who was quite jubilant about the Swift being completed within the time be had estimated, didn't appreciate my frame of mind. 'Why don't you get lost for a couple of days.' He counselled. 'Go down to Birmingham and take your aunts out to Sutton Park and feed the ducks,' He facetiously suggested.

'I might do that.' I replied.

'Well! Be back here in time to fly down to Lympne next Saturday morning. The Persian permit should be here by then.'

John Walker who had been listening to our dialogue then said he would be pleased if I went as far as Castle Bromwich with him. 'You fly the 'kite', then I can tell Comper what sort of a pilot you are.'

A trifle overcome by John Walker's generous invitation, I lost no time in climbing into the rear cockpit of his Moth. Seconds later we were southbound through a haze which had built up since I passed that way earlier.

My passenger puzzled me, for he was a man who differed considerably from my conception of a millionaire.

Although unconventional, it was, perhaps, understandable that one of those rare individuals should indulge in what most people thought to be, the risky art of flying, but to place his life and his aircraft in the hands of a stranger, was to say the least, very remarkable, to my way of thinking.

That millionaires lived in lofty isolation surrounded by and waited on by an army of flunkeys and who, when travelling rode in Rolls Royce cars, or in reserved carriages on express trains which were halted at private stations for the millionaire's particular convenience, but never in aeroplanes, was an impression which had been shattered by meeting Johnnie Walker who was undoubtedly the peer of the subject of Kipling's 'If '.

In less than an hour we arrived at Castle Bromwich where Johnnie Walker took over and continued on his way to London.

That was the first and the last time I met this charming and well known gentleman, but I never see a square bottle with a black or red label without being reminded of a pleasant afternoon spent in good company on 21st of October 1931.

By the time the Moth had disappeared into the haze hanging over the southeast environs of Birmingham my outlook on life had returned to normal.

Instead of proposing a visit to Sutton Park as Comper had suggested, I invited my aunts to spend the following day in London with me.

My younger aunt became quite excited about visiting the great metropolis which she hadn't seen for many years. Her sister, however was horrified by the idea of gallivanting about that city of sin as she termed it.

Next morning, after being briefed about pickpockets and other vagrants by my Aunt Eleanor who was an avid reader of Dickens, I took Aunt Emily off to Snow Hill station, catching the 8 o'clock train for Paddington with the intention of taking a leisurely tour of the Capital.

My aunt had other ideas. The leisurely jaunt I had envisaged became a marathon pilgrimage leading first to Kensington Gardens with its palace and statues, thence across the city via numerous places of interest (to my aunt) to the Tower. A trek which took over 6½ hours and covered approximately 14 miles, by my reckoning.

Now! A stroll of this distance through the Australian bush or the English countryside can be achieved without undue effort, however walking such a distance over hard pavements, in addition to climbing up and down innumerable steps enroute, is an entirely different matter, particularly when such a journey is undertaken without rest or refreshment.

Showing a determination quite foreign to her normal character, my aunt brushed aside my suggestion that it would be wise to take a cab, telling me the only way to thoroughly see a place is on foot, nor would my aunt listen to my pleas and finally my demands that we should stop for lunch or even a cup of tea.

When, at last, we boarded the train for the return journey, I was so footsore and weary as to be anxious about being fit for the long flight I was soon to undertake. Also I could not help admiring my aunt's fortitude and wondering what impelled her to behave as she had done during the whole of the time we had spent in London.

By the time the train reached Birmingham, the sprightly amazon had become a tired old lady who, no longer able to endure the torture of her boots, removed them in the taxi on the last stage of the journey.

Aunt Eleanor was not amused by her sister's unshod arrival. She upbraided me for bringing my aunt home in such a condition. I lacked the words and the will to offer an explanation and my Aunt Emily seemed most reluctant to disclose the unusual facet of her character which had been manifest in London.

Neither the scolding, nor my sore feet and aching limbs prevented me from sleeping better than I had done during the past few weeks.

Although disappointed, when I returned to Hooton on Friday afternoon, to find the Persian permit had failed to materialise, my spirits were revived somewhat by a letter from my lady love which had been sent on to Hooton from Australia House. A brief note acknowledging a post card from Colombo, which I had sent on my way to England.

During my absence the Swift had been flown with full load of fuel. The take off was so poor it was found necessary to replace the standard propeller by one having a finer pitch.

Unfortunately the cruising speed with the new propeller was slower by at least 15 miles per hour, although the takeoff performance improved considerably.

This decrease in the cruising speed would increase the flying time between Lympne and Tooraweenah (a small country town in NSW) by at least 14 hours. The still air range of the Swift would also be reduced by approximately 130 miles to 840 miles, making it obvious considerable alteration would have to be made to my itinerary. The first stage from Lympne to Rome was out. Instead I substituted Lympne, Marseille, Brindisi, aiming to land, by moonlight, at Athens about 9p.m. Regardless of having to fly an extra 2 hours 40 minutes between Athens and Karachi, I hoped to arrive at the latter place at the time set out originally, by leaving Athens earlier and spending less time on the ground at Aleppo. All the remaining stages were within range although the safety margin was less, so much so on some stages that a strong head wind would mean an additional stop to refuel.

Despite the slower and additional time, given fair weather I could still get to Tooraweenah 9 days after departure from Lympne, providing the Persian permit arrived by Monday.

Monday, the day after I was due to depart, was perfect weatherwise, not only on the Wirral, but over my projected route as far as Athens, according to the weather reports.

I left the Edye household early to be at the works in time for the arrival of the first post, but there was nothing in it for me.

With unkindly thoughts about Persian procrastination, I walked over to the hangars, intending to vent my feelings by taking G-AAZF (Nic Comper's Swift) aloft, only to find the aircraft being 'fussed over' by two engineers doing a maintenance check. The new Swift, G-ABRE looking beautiful in its coat of blue, with white edging and lettering, standing alongside, tempted me, but Nic Comper's edict, that it should not be flown before being taken to Lympne, made sense, because the engine would be due for overhaul by the time it reached Australia.

I decided to go for a walk, hoping the exercise would relieve my feelings. After tramping a couple of miles, my feet, which hadn't recovered from pounding the London pavements, started to protest, so I sat on a style thinking about the almost impossible feat which had been accomplished in preparing for the flight to Australia. An effort now likely to be jeopardised should the weather break.

Already there had been widespread fogs in England and France, but more important, from now on the moon would be on the wane and within a few days its light would be insufficient for night landings to be made without the aid of flares.

With no information available about night landing facilities at Athens and Basra, plans for landing at these places after dark would have to be abandoned unless I was able to start before Wednesday.

Had all gone according to plan, I should have now been in the vicinity of Aleppo instead of idling in the 'wilds' of the Wirral, so frustrated that even the sight of a few placid cows, chewing their cud, annoyed me so much I picked up a piece of dried dung and hurled at the nearest, hitting it on the rump.

Feeling rather ashamed of my childish behaviour I headed back to the aerodrome to await the next post. Fourteen days had elapsed since making an application to fly over Persia, plenty of time for those concerned to have attended to this matter.

Yet! Was it?

Persia was several thousand miles away and without knowing anything about the postal facilities of that country, it was, perhaps unfair to expect a speedy handling of the mail.

Imperial Airways flew over the south of Persia and probably called at Bushire or Jask, but so far as I knew, there were no railways linking these ports with Teheran. It was quite likely the mail in that part of the world was transported by donkeys or camels. A thought which made me realise there was every possibility that I might be awaiting the permit for another month or so.

The remainder of the day passed miserably. I checked and rechecked my course until sick of the sight of maps, I wandered aimlessly around until the postman made his last call for the day.

The first mail delivery next day, again brought nothing but disappointment. To fill in time before the next visit of the postman I took Nic Comper's Swift for a flight, but it was no pleasure, despite near perfect weather, to be flying without purpose over England, instead of speeding over Arabia, 3,000 miles on my way to Tooraweenah.

In due course, finding myself over Birmingham, I decided to drop in on my aunts for whom I had developed a real affection. They were surprised to see me, believing me to be on my way to Australia.

Aunt Emily was still suffering from the effects of our excursion to London. She had, however confessed to her sister that she alone had been responsible for her blistered feet.

On the way back to Hooton, the weather deteriorated, an indication of a breakup of the Indian summer and perhaps a warning that flying was not going to be so pleasant from now on.

Next day seemed interminable. The weather was too bad to fly or enjoy walking. Finding it impossible to read, I filled in time sitting in the cockpit of G-ABRE, imagining I was flying over India which I should have been doing had things gone as planned.

Then my mind switched to wondering what was happening at Tooraweenah, thoughts which dampened my spirit further and increased the tension. It was worse than waiting on the blocks at the start of a foot race, when the starter had forgotten to load his pistol.

The day ended with no sign of the permit. Even Nic Comper, who had, so far, been philosophical about the delay, was becoming impatient.

He decided we should fly down to Lympne next day, calling at London, where Comper intended to get some action from the Persians.

Uncle Frank and Aunt Freida came to the aerodrome to bid me farewell. My uncle presented me with a large pistol 'To fend off attacks by tigers or hostile tribes should you be menaced in the jungle or any other outlandish place,' he said. He was very disappointed when I declined to accept his prized possession. My aunt gave me a pair of carpet slippers, a small alarm clock and a large block of chocolate. The slippers proved a great boon until they were souvenired at Victoria Point. The alarm clock travelled as far as

Darwin, where it was also souvenired, and over Arabia the chocolate melted, pouring from its package to form a sticky mass on the cockpit floor.

Nic Comper flew the new Swift G-ABRE and I piloted his aircraft G-AAZF. Flying in formation, wingtip to wingtip, it was necessary to throttle Comper's aircraft well back to stay with the new machine whose cruising performance was rather disappointing. However it was far better for a bit of speed to be sacrificed than risk a crash taking off in some remote spot in the tropics.

In London the Persians were unmoved by Nic Comper's charm. We came away from their consulate without knowing if or when a permit would be granted.

I was all for setting out without more ado, but Nic Comper, although annoyed and disappointed, counselled patience.

'You will probably find yourself locked up in a Persian gaol perhaps for an indefinite period with every chance of the Swift being confiscated, if you land in Persia without the necessary documents,' he said.

Realising the futility of remaining in London we flew on to Lympne which had been selected as the point of departure for several reasons. It was the customs aerodrome nearest the continent, it had night flying facilities and, more important, it was less subject to fog than aerodromes in the London area. A favourite 'hopping off ' place for those bound for Australia, the East and for Africa.

Two brothers, Hamilton by name, had set out for Australia at an early hour that morning. Their aircraft having sufficient range to bypass Persia as Charles Scott had done earlier in the year.

The newspapers also reported that W. Aston, a dirt track rider by profession, and two others H. Jenkins and H. Jefferies were hoping to leave that week. All attempting to break the speed record to Australia.

The air road to the Antipodes was becoming quite crowded, this could be the reason for reluctance on the part of Persians to grant permission to land in their country.

Soon after our arrival at Lympne, James Jeffs, who was in charge of the aerodrome, checked my documents so that I would be able to depart with as little delay as possible after the Persian permit had been issued.

When he discovered I had no medical certificate other than the record of the date and result of medical examinations endorsed in my pilots licence, Jeffs advised me to obtain a medical certificate forthwith, otherwise there was every likelihood of my being held up enroute.

George Edye who had motored down from Cheshire, took me into Hythe, the nearest village to obtain a certificate. The doctor was not in his surgery, but we eventually ran him to earth at a 'pub' in the High Street, called 'The White Hart'. Here the doctor listened to my urgent plea for an examination and a certificate of health. He looked at my eyes, requested me to put out my tongue and asked me if I had been vaccinated, then taking a piece of hotel notepaper be wrote out a statement that I had been vaccinated, inoculated and was free from infection.

Refusing a fee, the doctor wished me luck and returned to his convivial companions.

James Jeffs raised his eyebrows when he saw the health certificate. 'That will need to appear more official otherwise its authenticity is likely to be challenged.' He said as he took a rubber stamp from his desk and imprinted Duty Office Lympne Airport' beneath the doctor's signature.

Next morning, 29th October, I prowled about the aerodrome like a cat in a cage until Nic Comper suggested I take G-ABRE aloft and practice instrument flying.

Owing to the size of the auxiliary petrol tank, it had been necessary to move the instrument board back so close to the pilot there was insufficient room to install a P.B. Deviator. A Reid Sigrist turn and bank indicator was fitted instead.

An altimeter, clock, airspeed indicator, engine revolution counter and oil gauge completed the panel The compass being installed on a bracket beneath the panel.

Compared to the standard Swift, G-ABRE with its full load was rather sluggish taking off and not so nice to handle when airborne, all the same, its performance was remarkable considering its all up weight was more than twice its standard tare weight of 543 lbs.

Prior to taking off, I carefully plotted a triangular course from Lympne over Ashford and Dungeness, thence back to Lympne, allowing for the forecast wind.

Resisting the temptation to take a periodical peep at the terrain below, I flew the course with my eyes glued to the instruments, finishing well out over the English Channel abeam of Hythe. Three times I took the Swift around the course with little better results.

Realising my blind flying ability left much to be desired, I consoled myself with this knowledge that the journey to Australia would be a series of straight flights.

The new instrument seemed satisfactory in the calm air presently prevailing, but it was so sensitive I was dubious of being capable of following its guidance in turbulent weather.

With its overload of fuel the Swift came in to land like a bat out of hell, its stalling speed having increased by at least 30%. This didn't worry me unduly, because the aircraft would be much lighter on future landings, unless engine failure occurred soon after takeoff.

During the remainder of the day, I filled in time checking over my revised schedule and bemoaning the loss of moonlight which would prevent me from landing at Athens and Basra after darkness had fallen.

Friday, the 30th, turned out to be a glorious day for doing things out of doors, especially flying. I felt tempted to ask Nic Comper to let me have his Swift for a trial run over the route as far as Paris and back, but it would have been just my luck for the Persian permit to have turned up whilst I was away.

When no word had been received by 10 o'clock, James Jeffs decided to contact the Air Ministry and request one of his colleagues to do something about the matter.

The monotony was broken later in the morning by the arrival of a 'Puss Moth' flown by a well known pilot Gordon Store and a girl Peggy Salaman. They planned to leave at midnight with the intention of breaking the record to Cape Town.

During the afternoon, time pushed the hands of the clock round seemingly slower and slower, until shortly after 5 o'clock, George Edye said he had had his fill of Lympne. 'We are not likely to hear from the Persians before Monday. My people are giving a house party during the weekend, I suggest we go over and join them.'

Edye's parents lived near Bibury in Gloucestershire, about 140 miles away.

Comper didn't like the idea neither did I. The only clothes I possessed, the old suit I was wearing, plus a change of underclothing were not exactly suitable for attending a fashionable party, besides there was a remote possibility of starting the flight during the weekend.

George Edye was still trying to persuade us to change our minds when a message came through from London. Thanks to the efforts of James Jeffs, permission to fly over Persia had been granted at last.

Although it was a relief to know the way to Australia was not unbarred, I was not overjoyed at leaving 6 days later than planned. Apart from being deprived of moonlight over the first stages, the prospect of encountering bad weather on the last stages had increased. Above all was my anxiety about what might be happening at Tooraweenah.

Retiring after an early dinner with the hope of getting a few hours sleep before my departure at half past midnight, I had reached that chimerical state which borders sleep, when Nic Comper aroused me with the news, the Vacuum Oil Company representative was unable to contact the Marseille office and was sure I would be delayed when I landed there at dawn to refuel. Reluctantly to delay my departure, I decided to refuel at Paris, which had full facilities for night operations and again at Rome.

The additional stop would retard my progress, nevertheless I should be able to reach Brindisi well before nightfall. Unfortunately this plan had to be abandoned because Le Bourget Airport was reported fogbound. It seemed that fate was against me.

With ill grace I accepted the advice of the oilman, to leave Lympne at 5am. This meant I would be hard pushed getting to Brindisi before the following night.

Except for a slight haze, which partly obscured the boundary lights at the far end of the aerodrome, conditions were perfect when I taxied away from the tarmac shortly before 5 o'clock on Saturday 31st October 1931.

Quite elated at the thought of seeing the lady I loved within a few days, I swung the Swift round to face the 3 knot zephyr coming in from the west, and opened up the throttle.

As the aircraft gathered speed, I received a sharp blow on my right thigh. Hastily closing the throttle, I glanced inside the cockpit wondering what had hit me. The luminous dial of the clock was missing from its place on the instrument board.

A trifle upset by this discovery, I taxied rapidly back to the tarmac, where Nic Comper came alongside the cockpit before I was able to shut off the engine, be bellowed 'What is the matter now?'

My terse retort 'Your blasted aeroplane is falling apart', brought a stunned silence.

Jumping from the cockpit, I removed my flying coat which I thrust into Comper's hands after taking a torch from its pocket.

Diving head first into the cockpit, I located and retrieved the clock and its lock ring from the cockpit floor.

Within 5 minutes the clock had been refitted, none the worse for its fall, and I was taxying back to the takeoff point.

The clock showed exactly 5.10 as I pushed the throttle wide the second time. The Swift again gathered speed, the wheels finally parting company with the soil of England and a few seconds later the red boundary lights of the aerodrome shot by beneath the machine.

Ten precious minutes had been lost and my nervous system well nigh shattered. However, the Swift was, at last, on its way to Australia, climbing slowly into the predawn darkness.

At 1,000 feet, I brought the aircraft round on course for Marseille, heading out over the English Channel for France, still hopeful of reaching Brindisi before nightfall.

Over the water, the haze disappeared, revealing the flashing light on Cap Gris Nez, far away to the left on the French coast. On the Channel below, the green, red and white lights of ships passed beneath the climbing aircraft, some, perhaps, bound for Australia.

The lights of Boulogne were abreast, about 20 miles to the east, twenty minutes after takeoff, indicating the Swift was making good progress. A quarter of an hour later the Swift was over the mouth of the Somme, its first sea crossing accomplished. By now, the stars in the east were beginning to pale, heralding the coming of dawn.

Gradually the earth became distinct. The fields of France lined with Poplars appearing ethereal in the first light of day. Then fog came blotting the land ahead as far as the eye could see.

The Sun rose as the Swift came abreast of Paris, clearly indicated by the Eiffel Tower projecting from fog enshrouded city.

A few miles north of Lyon, the fog dispersed revealing the beautiful Saone and Rhone valleys, their lush meadows fringed by vine clad slopes, a scene enhanced by the snow capped Alps silhouetted on the eastern horizon nearly 100 miles away. A silhouette which reminded me of the rugged grandeur of the Warrumbungles in whose foothills my ultimate destination lay.

Exactly 5 hours after departure, Marseille appeared ahead and 10 minutes later the Swift was skimming the turn on Marignane aerodrome. Thanks to a tail wind, the first leg of my flight had been covered at an average speed of 114 miles per hour. Maintaining this rate of progress I should be able to reach Brindisi that night and have no difficulty in traversing the remaining 8,900 miles within the time planned.

Whilst the Swift was being refuelled, I hastened to the Customs Office expecting an immediate clearance and to be on my way within a few minutes.

The sole Customs officer had other ideas. After checking my documents, he asked my ultimate destination and next port of call. 'Australia via Brindisi' I replied.

Picking up my passport which he had already examined thoroughly he turned to page 17 and pointing, demanded. 'If so why do you require a Portuguese visa?'

My explanation, that I might be compelled to land at Dilli in Portuguese Timor, fell on deaf ears. My interrogator had vanished into another part of the building, taking my passport with him.

I had now been on the ground for more than 10 minutes. G-ABRE had been refuelled and I was ready to leave as soon as my documents were returned.

The minutes dragged by without a sign of the customs fellow, each minute lessening my chances of reaching Brindisi that day and sending my blood pressure up to an uncomfortable level.

I was telling myself to keep calm, when the customs officer returned. Instead of giving me a clearance, he went over to the Swift and commenced removing the engine cowlings.

'Eh! What is the idea?' I demanded.

'Contraband' was the reply.

'The aircraft is not carrying any contraband', I said heatedly.

'We shall see', the customs fellow said as he felt behind the engine.

After inspecting the engine bay, the examiner turned his attention to the cockpit, whilst I replaced the engine cowls. The cockpit search proved fruitless, but as the fellow was getting out of the cockpit he noticed the pilot's headrest was detachable. With a cry of satisfaction, he removed the cover only to find the engine tool kit clipped to the back. With obvious disappointment, he replaced the cover, then opened the rear locker in which a water tank had been fitted for emergencies. After sampling the water, the searcher gave up and returned to the office to search my attache case, which contained 2 pairs of sox, two shirts, a set of underwear, tooth brush, razor, alarm clock, the tube of food tablets and the block of chocolate, all of which were examined carefully as were the bottom and sides of the case. The customs fellow seemed reluctant to let me go. To my surprise, he invited me to take coffee with him.

I declined, saying I had a long way to go and must be on my way.

The customs man then stamped my passport and carnet, whilst I repacked my case.

Running out to the Swift, I got the aircraft airborne as soon as possible, but it was rather a futile gesture, because leaving Marignane 50 minutes later than I should have done there seemed little chance of reaching Brindisi that night.

As the Swift came round on course the sight of Marseille dominated by Notre Dame du la Garde brought vivid memories of the day spent in this city on my way to England. A day on which the local citizens were celebrating, with exhausting fervor, the anniversary of the canonization of one of their saints.

With a shipboard acquaintance (a staid member of the Colonial Service returning to his homeland from Ceylon) I had set out to explore the city immediately the ship docked. Soon we were caught up in a vast crowd of religious devotees making a pilgrimage to Notre Dame du la Garde.

After being impressed with the holy aspect of Marseille, we were fated to be shown the shadier side of the city. It began in the Rue de la Cannebiere - now almost beneath the nose of the Swift - along which we headed with the intention of taking a tram ride along the coast from the terminus near the Inner Port.

As we strolled along la Cannebiere, my companion responding to an urgent call of nature entered a cafe, leaving me on the pavement observing the townsfolk promenading in their holiday attire.

Out of the throng a well dressed man appeared and after bidding me good day, asked if I was enjoying my visit to the city. A conversation ensued during which the local citizen learned of my interest in French art, particularly the works of Watteau.

The Frenchman enthusiastically said he had a few objects d'art he was sure I would be interested in. The return of my shipboard acquaintance interrupted our talk, whereupon the Frenchman invited us to call on him on our return from our trip along the coast. He delved into his pocket, then apologising for not having a visiting card, he asked us to accompany him to his house a short distance away. A few minutes walk brought us to an imposing residence, where our potential host led us into an elegantly furnished hall dominated by an imposing staircase up which our host disappeared to return a few seconds later with a card which I placed in my pocket without so much as a glance.

'Au revoir until tonight' floated after us as we departed.

My companion until now had maintained a stony silence, but as soon as we were clear of the Frenchman's mansion he exploded 'If you intend to spend the night in a cathouse, you can count me out. I am a respectable man, I thought you were also'.

This outburst astonished me, I could see nothing wrong in accepting an invitation from a friendly art lover to view his objects d'art, as he called them. In fact, if they were in keeping with his somewhat pretentious residence, they should be well worth seeing. I said as much to my companion, who replied. 'You Australians are very naive. That place is a brothel if ever I saw one, and I am not in the habit of patronising brothels.'

'Surely you must be mistaken,' I said as I brought forth the Frenchman's card. It was embossed thus:

Madame de Pertuis. Maitresse Directeur
ECOLE DU JEUNE FILLES
Rue ....
Marseille
Discretion

Very upset, I boarded the tram on the wrong side (which is the correct side in Australia) apparently a grave transgression in Marseille, because a gesticulating conductor verbally assailed us with a torrent of abuse, only one word of which we understood 'Imbeciles'.

Acutely embarrassed we sat silently while the tram carried us towards its destination where unfortunately further embarrassment awaited us.

The tram, after frequent stops to pick up gaily dressed people arrived at its destination, Sebastapol, crammed to capacity. As it slowed to a stop, its excited passengers were leaping off to join a large crowd gathered round a group of young people dancing to the sound of wild, melodious music coming from an accordion and two violins played by musicians on a platform perched on the top of a pole in the centre of the village square.

There was nothing sedate about the dancers, the males tossing their partners about like rag dolls, nevertheless, in a pattern in keeping with the music. It was like a colourful scene from a musical comedy, only far more exciting.

We were gradually making our way through the crowd, when suddenly alongside us, someone yelled. 'Viola! Brigand!'. The crowd scattered as knives flashed.

'Let us get out of here' my companion cried as he made for the tram as fast as the crowd would allow. I followed expecting to receive a knife in my back at any second.

From the tram, which was rapidly filling with gesticulating escapees from the fighting, shouting mob, we watched the meleé. The musicians and dancers, apparently oblivious to the disturbance continued with wild abandon even after the arrival of a number of police who soon quietened the mob. Then two policemen entered the tram, surveying the now silent occupants, whilst conversing with the conductor, afterwards moving along the corridor until they were alongside us.

Watched by our fellow passengers, probably anticipating an arrest, we were subjected to intense scrutiny by the gendarmerie. After a seemingly lengthy and silent survey, which caused me to blush with embarrassment, one of the policemen leaned over, his garlic laden breath enveloping us as his spate of words broke the silence.

Almost immediately, his voice was drowned by sounds of renewed violence in the square. The policemen rushed out of the tram which moved off immediately, to the obvious disappointment of some of the passengers, who continued to cast suspicious glances in our direction.

Arriving back in the city without further incident, about 8pm we dined at a small cafe near the docks. As we were finishing our meal, the proprietor attempted to persuade us to visit a place of entertainment which he said would be an education of a lifetime.

His vivid description of the 'delights' we would experience quite upset my companion, who jumped up saying as he did so. 'Let us get out of this den of sin'.

On the way back to the ship I was given a lecture on the immorality of the French by my disgusted companion. Thus ended the day previously spent in Marseille, which had now faded astern.

By the time the Swift crossed the coast near Cap Lardier it was obvious the wind, which had been on my tail during the first leg, had now veered to the east.

As the Swift headed out over the sea I began to feel afraid. A feeling which grew as the coast gradually faded away on my left. Soon I felt I couldn't go on, but thoughts of what people would say when they learned I had flunked my first flight of any distance across water created another fear, that of ridicule.

While these two facets of fear battled for possession of my mind, the land disappeared entirely and with it my fears, leaving me a trifle apprehensive, may be, yet no longer sweating at the palms.

I was now alone in the world of blue. Azure canopy above, unblemished by a single cloud, and an ultramarine disc below. The impression that the aircraft was trapped between two saucers whose rims met on the horizon, gave me a slight feeling of claustrophobia, also a sense of loneliness.

Hoping to find a wind more favourable at a higher altitude, I climbed the Swift until the altimeter registered 10,000 feet. At this height, the snow capped Alps showed briefly, etched on the northern horizon. Before long a haze gathered in the atmosphere. This restriction of visibility gave the impression the Swift was stationary. Only the icy blast of the slipstream on my face and the gyrating second of the clock indicated movement, even the noise of the engine seemed muted, adding to the unreal feeling of immobility.

After enduring this irritating experience for more than half an hour, I eased the nose of the Swift down, seeking a lower and warmer altitude. Then another nuisance, hunger made itself felt. Over 9 hours had elapsed since I had swallowed anything. The tea and toast consumed prior to leaving England no longer sustained me. Unfortunately the chocolate given to me by my aunt and the emergency food tablets were in the case in the back locker.

For some time thoughts of food were paramount, my imagination setting out many delectable dishes, which I might choose for my next meal.

Thoughts interrupted suddenly, when I realised that over 1 hour had elapsed since leaving the French coast, ample time to have crossed the 135 miles of that part of the Mediterranean, named the Ligurian Sea. Corsica should have been reached before now. Either the wind which had slowed the Swift between Marseille and Cape Lardier, had increased substantially or the Swift had drifted so far north of its course, it had missed Corsica altogether.

Assuming the latter to be the case, I altered course a few degrees to the starboard, hoping this would bring the Swift back on track by the time the Italian coast was reached.

Several minutes later a rocky coast loomed out of the haze about 4 miles ahead. Landfall had been made at Gulf St Florent, a few miles north of my track.

Cloud enveloped the mountainous backbone of Corsica, forming fantastic castles in the air above the range which at the northern end of the island, forms a long narrow peninsula pointing like a finger to the Gulf of Genoa.

In less than ten minutes the Swift had crossed this cloud enshrouded part of the island and was abreast of Bastia, a picturesque town basking in the Sun about two miles away to the port.

Checking time and distance since leaving Marseille revealed the surface speed of the Swift had been no more than 85 miles per hour. At this speed, another 5 hours would elapse before Brindisi could be reached which meant arriving well after nightfall and according to my estimate with less than three gallons of fuel in the tanks. Something I didn't relish. It appeared I would have to stay the night at Rome, beyond which the terrain was mountainous with no landing grounds marked on the map.

By the time I had reviewed my position, the Swift was over the island of Pianosa, the haze had cleared and the island of Elba showed about ten miles to the north. Then the island of Monte appeared the same distance away to the south, with Gigli ahead. It was remarkable how the sight of these islands boosted the morale, although they were beyond reach should the engine fail.

The Swift reached the Italian coast eighty minutes after passing Bastia. Twenty minutes later Rome came in sight. The ancient city aglow in the rays of the setting sun presented a sight of indescribable beauty.

As the aircraft lost height over the city, I noticed the wind at ground level was from the north. Having had an hour to spare before sunset, with the tailwind it should be possible to travel another 100 miles, at least, before nightfall, a temptation too strong to resist.

Feeling sure I would find a suitable paddock in which to land somewhere down the Liri Valley, I opened up the throttle, heading the Swift over the Alban Hills and down into the Kin Valley beyond.

The aircraft was approaching Ponticorvo when the sun disappeared behind the Lepini Mountains, going down in a blaze of glory beyond the

Tyrrhenian Sea. A multitude of small fields unfolded along the valley, none suitable for landing, and as daylight faded my anxiety rapidly grew.

Already night had cast it mantle over the Appennines towering to the east and the terrain below was becoming indistinct, with no signs of a place to land.

Faced with either flying approximately 80 miles back to Rome or continuing to Brindisi, I chose the latter. The weather was fine and clear, and at its present rate of progress the Swift should arrive over Brindisi with sufficient fuel to fly for another hour, at least. Ample to find the aerodrome before fuel was exhausted.

As I climbed the Swift to clear the Matese Range, the peaks of which rise to well over 6,000 feet, a feeling of lassitude suddenly assailed me. By the time 8,000 feet was reached, I was feeling extremely fatigued although I had flown less than eleven hours since leaving England.

Apart from the likelihood of becoming so tired as to be incapable of finding the aerodrome and making a landing after flying for another two hours, what really worried me was the possibility I might not have the physical and mental capacity to maintain the schedule I had planned. Yet, having previously flown 13 hours in a period of 14 hours, without fatigue, under conditions much worse than experienced today, I wondered if I was succumbing to some malady.

These morbid thoughts were interrupted when I spotted the lights of a large city far to the south and outside the area covered by my map.

Like a moth attracted to a flame I headed towards the city, hoping that I would be able to find a landing place.

Twenty minutes later I was over the outskirts of what I guessed to be Naples, seeking signs of an aerodrome. In vain I searched for red boundary lights, a lighted windsock or an aircraft in front of a hangar.

If an aerodrome existed here it seemed that it wasn't used at night.

Acute anxiety drove away my fatigue when I realised, that by now, there was insufficient fuel in the aircraft to return to Rome or reach Brindisi, and that before long, the Swift would be forced down to earth.

Attempting a landing in the countryside was not likely to be successful, the possibility of damaging the property of some poor farmer and the risk of killing someone, ruled out this idea.

Three alternatives remained. I might be able to find a straight, well lit road, clear of traffic and overhead wires, on which a landing could be made.

The second alternative was a suitable beach, and as a last resort, ditching the Swift in the bay.

There were several well lit roads threading the city, all containing too much traffic. One particularly well lit thoroughfare, running parallel to and near the coast, straight for half a mile or more and wide enough for three Swifts to be landed abreast, was a great temptation, but thoughts of the consequences should the landing be unsuccessful, restrained me from making an attempt.

Darkness hid the beaches, if there were any, along the shores of the Bay of Naples, leaving only one alternative, the waters of the Bay. Disliking the idea of ditching, I decided to delay the inevitable by staying aloft until the fuel ran out.

That I was happy with the turn of events would be a gross exaggeration. Yet! strange to say, I no longer felt frightened or fatigued as I took the Swift up to a safer height after my fruitless search.

Now that I was aware of the exact position, it was almost with relief I faced the challenge of getting back to earth with a whole skin.

From 4,000 feet, the mass of lights below looked quite active but it was the dark stretch of water to the south of the lights which held my interest. Finally, I decided to put the Swift down alongside a flashing light not far from the shore, hoping the aircraft would remain afloat until someone rescued me or would drift to within six or seven yards of the shore. The limit of my capacity as a 'dog paddler'.

It was useless to deplore the fact that I never learned to swim properly or to dwell on the folly which had caused the situation leading to my present embarrassment. It served me right.

When I had first flown over the city, I had seen, well within its limits, an unlit area of considerable size which I had assumed to be a park with trees and other obstacles precluding a safe landing.

The thought now occurred to me, that if this park contained a pond, even of modest dimensions, it might be possible to stall the Swift into it, without too much damage being done.

With most of the fuel used, the stalling speed of the aircraft would be comparatively slow. Also there was a possibility of the engine escaping damage, a certainty if it was immersed in salt water. Another thing, was the chance of the pond, if one existed, being shallow enough for me to wade out of it.

In a more optimistic frame of mind, I wasted no time in making a gliding approach to the park. Flying over the area as low as I dared and scanning the black void for some indication of star reflection which would surely show if there was any water below.

Nothing was visible on that featureless carpet of jet black, not even a variation of density one would expect if there were trees and bushes growing on the area.

Reconciling myself to the inevitable, I pulled the Swift into a climb back to safer altitude, as I did so I noticed along one of the boundaries of the park, a tramline along which trams were travelling frequently, their light showing up a tall fence of iron railings and a strip of ground inside the park which seemed clear of obstructions as far as the lights reached.

Hoping there were no trees out of range of the lights which might snag a wing, I decided to put the Swift down as close to the fence as possible.

It is not easy to judge height and distance by the light from a moving tram, a discovery I made when starting my final glide to land.

After maneuvering into a position to overtake a tram already on its way alongside the boundary fence, I attempted to touch down as the Swift drew level with the light from the tram, for a fleeting second I saw the ground, as the Swift sped past into the darkness.

Tense with anticipation I waited for what seemed an interminable time before the wheels touched, skipped, touched again then ran smoothly. The tram rattled by momentarily lighting the scene before darkness came again. The aircraft, having no brakes rolled on and on, gradually slowing, then just as I was congratulating myself on a safe return to earth, the Swift struck an obstruction which swung it round to a standstill.

Jumping out of the cockpit to investigate, I found a man sprawled on the ground beneath the port wing. Helping him to his feet I asked 'Are you hurt?' Instead of replying, he snatched his arm from my grasp and ran off into the darkness.

This behaviour puzzled me until I realised that to be felled without warning and afterwards addressed in a foreign tongue would be rather alarming.

After attending to an urgent call of nature, I commenced walking in the direction my victim had taken, hoping to find a way out of the park.

I had gone no more than a few yards when a searchlight was switched on from a spot away on my right. The light after sweeping the area, which appeared to be quite large and free from obstacles, finally settled on the Swift.

Returning to the aircraft I restarted the engine and taxied along the beam of light, eventually arriving on a tarmac fronting an extensive block of buildings, where a gesticulating crowd, attempting to approach the Swift was being held in check by a number of soldiers.

The shouting and struggling crowd nearly broke through the cordon, as I got out of the cockpit. My first thought was that the man I had skittled, bent on revenge, had raised this rabble. A foolish thought because it would have been impossible for this to have been done in so short a time.

Further cogitation was cut by an irate officer shouting at me in a foreign language which I assumed to be Italian. My request that he address me in English, briefly interrupted his diatribe which then continued with increased tempo. The crowd became silent, whilst I stood like a clot, feeling foolish and embarrassed, silently cursing the Tower of Babel as the officer continued to castigate me.

At last, in despair, I held up my hand, turned to the crowd, which had gradually edged closer, shouted an appeal for someone who could speak English.

The silence which followed was broken by a feminine voice answering my entreaty and out of the crowd came a young lady with an escort.

After a brief conversation with the person who had been shouting at me, the young lady addressed me in beautiful English. 'Lieutenant .... (I didn't catch his name) wishes to know who you are? From where you have come. What you are doing here and why did you arrive after nightfall?'

My answers were relayed to the lieutenant and in return I was told I had no right to land on a military aerodrome without permission, nor to be flying in darkness.

During the translation of this reprimand another officer appeared. He and lieutenant having a discussion and casting suspicious glances in my direction. The curiosity of those within range of the conversation turned to hostility, even the charming interpreter looked serious as she put the next question. 'Why did you land at Napoli if you were flying from Great Britain to Austria?'

Austria! Hundreds of miles to the north, little wonder the local lads thought I was up to a bit of no good. May be, a spy trying to sneak into the country under cover of darkness.

'I am flying to Australia not Austria', I explained.

When interpreted this statement met with a mixed reception. Some of the crowd laughed derisively. One old man, pointing, first to the Swift, then to me, tapped his head cackling as be did so. 'Australie! Australie!', much to my embarrassment, and the amusement of his companions.

The officers were not amused. A brusque order from one of them, relayed somewhat more kindly by the girl, to accompany them made me feel rather apprehensive.

The girl appeared to be enjoying her role as interpreter, her boy friend however, seemed impatient for the business to end. I was also tired of this seemingly endless interrogation, although I rather enjoyed the presence of the silver tongued, dark eyed beauty with raven hair, who had come to my aid.

As we followed the two officers I complimented the young lady on her excellent command of English and learned she had been educated at an English school.

There were several officers in the large room to which we were escorted, but none could speak English. Here I was told my story was disbelieved, because it was considered the Swift was incapable of making the journey to Australia.

My documents were demanded and whilst these were being perused, I produced my maps. Most of those present were more interested in these than in my passport, carnet and licences.

After much discussion, shaking of heads and waving of hands, the atmosphere became less frigid. The girl told me my story had been accepted, although most of those present, particularly the pilots thought I was very unwise.

My papers were handed back and I was invited to the mess for refreshments. I accepted providing the girl was included in the invitation, this caused some amusement to those present, excepting the interpreter's boy friend, who seemed rather displeased.

During the next half an hour, I answered many questions about my flight, the Swift and Australia. On my part I asked for the Swift to be refuelled and for arrangements to be made for me to leave Naples at midnight, so that I would be able to arrive at Athens at dawn tomorrow.

Refuelling would be attended to, but I would not be permitted to depart before daylight, because it was too dangerous to fly over the Apennines in the dark, I was told.

This edict, which made it impossible for me to reach Aleppo before nightfall, meant spending the following night on the Island of Rhodes or somewhere in Turkey. My thoughts on this subject were interrupted by the girl telling me I had been invited to dine with the officers.

My plea for her to be included in the invitation met with a strong protest from her escort. I suspected the young man of thinking I had amorous designs on his girl friend, whereas my sole interest was in her linguistic ability. Presenting me with his card, he hurriedly took the girl away.

I was sorry to see her depart because by the time dinner was over, I was mentally exhausted from the efforts at conducting conversation by sign language. The meal, however was excellent.

Dinner was served at a large table presided over by a tall distinguished looking gentleman with grey hair and sweeping moustache, which reminded me of photographs of General von Hindenberg.

It had been my intention to look over the Swift before leaving the aerodrome, but my hosts failed to understand my mimed request in this respect. Instead I was escorted to a car which took me to the Grand Hotel.

Although very tired, my first concern was the removal of the grease and grime I had collected since leaving England. Unfortunately there was no soap in either the palatial bedroom or the adjoining bathroom.

The crone who answered the service bell knew no English. However, after considerable pantomiming on my part, she produced a slab of something which could have been a piece of vintage parmesan cheese for all the lather it produced or grease it removed.

Next morning I was at the aerodrome well before daybreak. The Swift had been refuelled, but day had dawned before I finished checking the aircraft.

There were no signs of damage from the collision nor any complaints from the fellow involved, he had presumably kept quiet about the incident.

The sun came up over the Apennines as the Swift gained height over the fissure scarred slopes of Mount Vesuvius. A plume of smoke drifting from its peak tempted me to fly over the crater. A temptation I resisted.

Ahead the Apennines towered over the vine clad foothills dotted with quaint houses. A scene which soon gave way to more rugged views. In less than half an hour the mountains had given way to the plains of Puglia sloping away to the Gulf of Otranto just visible on the southern horizon, and in less than two hours Brindisi had slipped by a few miles to the north.

The Swift was making such good time I had visions of reaching Aleppo before the day faded, but that was not to be.

Conditions were perfect as the Swift sped out over the Adriatic. The sort of days 'a young man's fancy lightly turns to love', a state of bliss suddenly shattered by the smell of burning rubber.

Adversity, trouble, misfortune - call it what you will - inflicts itself in many ways. Sometimes coming with the speed of summer lightning, at others it is heralded gradually, so gradually indeed, it is at first taken for a figment of the imagination, as I did when that pungent smell invaded my nostrils on that Sabbath morning.

Not a wisp of smoke could be seen as I scanned the sea below for signs of a steamer or other cause for this odour. The surface was devoid of shipping. When I glanced behind for signs of smoke trailing the aircraft, the air was so clear the coast of Italy could still be seen, about to disappear beneath the horizon.

The engine had never run better, its oil pressure was normal and the other instruments steady, yet! despite the fact that all seemed well, the unusual smell made me uneasy.

Already the mountains of Albania and Greece were poking their peaks above the horizon ahead and the point of no return approaching rapidly, when a faint wisp of smoke appeared in the cockpit. Fire!

Previously I had faced the threat of incineration, when an aircraft, in which I was a passenger, caught fire. The prompt action of the pilot, in shutting off the petrol and sideslipping the machine into a convenient paddock saved our lives, but the terror of those few seconds remained imprinted on my memory.

Literally caught between the devil and the deep blue sea, I whipped the Swift round in a steep turn, heading back to the nearest land, hoping I might be able to get down before the aircraft became an inferno.

There was still no sign of fire within the cockpit, but as the minutes ticked by, the smoke increased, apparently leaking through the fireproof bulkhead from the bay behind the engine. Whatever the trouble, it was evident nothing could be done about the matter while the aircraft was in the air. The question was whether the fire, which, if the continuous increase of smoke was any indication, must be increasing, would set the fuel and oil alight before the shore was reached.

My thoughts were tinged with fear, as I tried to visualise in detail the layout of the bay behind the engine and the probable cause of the fire and its site in relation to the fuel and oil pipelines, and wondering how much heat these would withstand.

Within a few more minutes the smoke had become quite thick and the smell of burning wood with that of rubber.

Expecting to see the front of the aircraft become a mass of flame at any second, I considered ditching the Swift, but the engine was still running perfectly, pulling the aircraft towards the Italian coast, now clearly defined, not more than ten miles away.

Urged by fear, I pushed the throttle open as far as it would go. The engine responded, but the vibration was so great, I quickly reduced power to normal, pushing the nose of the machine down as I did so.

By the time the Swift was down to 2,000 feet and approximately 5 miles from land, smoke was seeping through behind my goggles making my eyes smart, forcing me to put my head out of the cockpit.

At last, the coast was within gliding distance of land with what appeared clear ground beyond. Suddenly the Swift shuddered. Horrified I glanced down through the smoke into the cockpit expecting to see the petrol tank, between my knees, in the process of disintegration and enveloped in flame, but there was nought but smoke swirling up and out of the cockpit.

The Swift shuddered again, buffeted by turbulence, often present where land meets sea.

The coast slid by 50 feet or so beneath, then the Swift was skimming the turn as I cut the switches and eased the stick back.

Grabbing the fire extinguisher clipped to the side of the cockpit, I jumped from the machine as it came to a stop and running to the front of the aircraft, whipped off the cowling covering the bay at the back of the engine. As the cowl came away, flames burst forth to be extinguished within a few seconds.

Very little damage had been done considering the time elapsing since I noticed the smell of burning rubber. It was amazing the Swift did not burn up in the air, why it didn't was probably due to lack of air at the site of the fire while the aircraft was in flight.

A considerable amount of the insulation covering the high tension lead from the port magneto to the distributor had been burned so had the ash strut to which the lead was clipped.

It did not take long to locate the cause of the trouble. A carbon brush in the distributor head had broken because the head had moved out of alignment, owing to someone tampering with the engine at Naples.

Fortunately Doctor Pobjoy had presented me with a compact engine kit which included a set of 4 brushes. I hoped to find sufficient high tension cable locally to replace the damaged lead, perhaps a garage, if such a place existed in this part of the country.

Without removing the engine nothing could be done about the damaged strut, but after careful examination I decided it would be safe unless I made a heavy landing.

I was so intent on examining the damage, I was unaware the aircraft had been surrounded by a curious crowd of men in uniform, until one of them tapped me on the shoulder and addressed me in Italian.

In response to my miming, I was thrust aside by several of the men, who after a discussion about the damage, commenced pushing the Swift towards a building about half a mile away, which I realised was a hangar. By the grace of God I had landed on another Italian military aerodrome.

On the tarmac, men swarmed round the Swift like ants round a wounded meat fly. With difficulty I pushed my way through the crowd to find a technician busy binding the damaged lead with insulating tape, making a very neat job which he completed within a few minutes.

The cowling was replaced, and thanking my benefactor, who understood not one word of my appreciation, I started the engine and commenced taxying away to takeoff, when a hefty soldier rushed over and grabbed a wingtip, swinging the Swift round in a circle.

Puzzled, I stopped the engine and stepped out of the cockpit, to be seized and escorted to an office, where an officer ranted at me in Italian.

Assuming he was demanding my papers which were in the rear locker of the Swift, I attempted to leave the room to get them.

Again I was seized and taken to another room. Frustrated by not knowing the reason for my incarceration, I again cursed the Tower of Babel.

The way things were shaping, I was doomed to spend an indefinite time in this forsaken place.

I prowled round and round the room trying to think of some way out of my predicament, regretting for the first time in my life, the lack of attention paid to the patient teacher who tried to instill me with Latin, during my school days.

The only window in the room was barred, but the door, when I tried to open it, I found unlocked. Quietly opening it enough to squeeze though, I crept into the corridor to find a guard facing me, a hefty fellow too large to tackle, even had I intended to do so. He waved me back.

Thinking quickly I told him I wanted to 'spend a penny'. He responded by pushing me back into the room. I then tried to get my message through by pantomime. An act misunderstood by the guard, who looked first amazed, then angry. Without a word he slammed the door in my face, leaving me to continue prowling round the room.

When it became obvious the idea of escaping was hopeless, my thoughts turned to other matters. Particularly food, with nothing to eat or drink since the previous night I was feeling rather empty and would have given almost anything for a cup of tea laced with plenty of milk, but I was reluctant to disturb the guard who would surely misinterpret my intentions.

Fingering the tube of food tablets which I had transferred to my flying coat pocket before leaving Naples, I debated with myself whether or not to break the seal.

In all there were 35 tablets, sufficient sustenance for 12 days according to Boots, the manufacturers.

After resisting temptation for nearly half an hour, I sampled a tablet, which with its faint flavour of malt was pleasant to taste.

It was difficult to swallow the soggy paste which formed as the tablet disintegrated in my mouth, but the eventual result was effective, although the bloated feeling which replaced hunger was rather uncomfortable.

About 3 hours after my arrival I was taken back to the office where an English speaking civilian questioned me, examined my papers, and after some discussion with the officer who had been responsible for my detention, reprimanded me for landing on a military aerodrome without permission. Finally my passport and carnet were stamped and I was ordered to leave immediately.

As I climbed into the cockpit, a soldier rushed over and thrust a piece of garlic sausage into my hand, a kindly deed which to some extent alleviated the inhospitality of those in authority and the annoyance caused by the delay which had cost me nearly 4 hours of perfect flying weather.

The Swift took off, climbing into the clear calm air and the tension of the past few hours disappeared. Although imprisoned for such a short period, my detention caused me to appreciate, for the first time, the joy of freedom which can only be valued fully by those who have been forcibly confined.

Despite the delay and the terrifying incident which had caused this, I became quite cheerful as the Swift sped out over the Gulf of Ontranto towards the mountains of Greece silhouetted on the horizon ahead.

I fished out the garlic sausage from my pocket and sampled the grubby looking fare. It tasted terrible, so I tossed it over the side for the fish.

Forty five minutes after departure from Italy the Swift was over the island of Corfu and running in to turbulence caused by a strong northerly wind which seemed to be increasing in velocity as the Swift headed over the barren ranges on the mainland.

I climbed the aircraft to 8,000 feet, hoping to find calmer air, but the aircraft continued to bound about like a bucking brumby. One second rocketing skyward, the next plunging towards the rugged terrain below. First on one wingtip then on the other, experiencing its first taste of severe turbulence.

Rather concerned about the likelihood of this continuous, violent buffeting causing the collapse of the damaged strut, I climbed the Swift higher hoping to find calmer air.

At 10,000 feet the air wasn't much smoother. By now, the intense cold numbed my hands and feet and made me very thankful when Athens, cradled by mountains and scattered with the remains of ancient architecture, eventually appeared. The starkness of the metropolis, fanning out south and southwest to the sea, relieved by the dark verdure of cypress trees.

The Swift, buffeted by a 50 knot gale, touched down at Tatoi aerodrome, a few miles north of Athens, at little more than walking pace. It would have probably been blown over on to its back had not two sailors grabbed the wing tips as soon as the aircraft landed and guided it into the lee of a hangar.

Getting out of the Swift with difficulty, I stood hanging to the cockpit combing, stamping my frozen feet to start the blood circulating again, whilst I watched the approach of a naval officer.

'Here it goes again', I thought 'You have no right to land without permission. Where have you come from? Where are you going? Where are your documents?' I was fed up with these inquisitions every time I landed.

The officer reached me, held out his hand and said 'I expect you could do with a cup of tea'.

I gaped at the young sub-lieutenant for several seconds before thanking him. This welcome was rather overwhelming after the receptions I had received on my arrivals in France and Italy.

However, to be greeted in such a friendly and civilised manner was, I suppose, only to be expected in this country, which after all, was the cradle of our civilization.

I was taken to a room in a block of offices nearby, where my escort excused himself, leaving me walking up and down stamping my feet and swinging my arms to get back some feeling in them. I had never been so cold.

Apart from cold and hunger, my shoulders were sore from being chafed by the Sutton harness during the turbulent flight from Corfu. Thoughts of the slow progress made so far, added to my misery.

Nearly two days to cover a mere 1650 miles and already I was feeling exceedingly tired, tired enough to consider abandoning the flight. What use was there, in trying to do something beyond my capacity? I asked myself.

Even if I eventually reached my goal, there was no certainty that my endeavours would be rewarded. The lady I loved might even think me ridiculous for making the attempt.

The damaged strut would be sufficient excuse for giving up the flight.

My brooding was interrupted by a naval rating bringing me tea and cakes. He was escorted by a fox terrier prancing along at his heels.

It is remarkable how irrelevant things become impressed upon the mind. An unusual cloud formation, a piece of paper snatched skyward by a gust of wind, even the antics of a capering canine.

The sailor deposited the refreshments on a table and departed. Not so the dog. It sat and watched me speculatively whilst I poured a cup of tea. When I reached for a cake, the dog came over and after butting my leg, sat up begging for a share.

Failing to achieve the desired result, the dog rolled on to its back.

Ignoring this overture, I rapidly consumed the first cake, it was so delicious I took another. The dog not to be denied stood on its hind legs and walked to the table, placing its paws on the edge, looking at the cakes then at me. I nearly weakened, but I was empty and in greater need of sustenance than an overfed dog.

The terrier repeated its performance with such persistence I eventually relented, giving a cake to the dog which made off immediately.

The perseverance so impressed me, I dismissed the craven idea of abandoning the flight, instead I decided to get away from Athens in time to arrive at Aleppo at the crack of dawn the following morning.

By the time I checked over the engine and examined the damaged strut - which appeared to have stood up to the buffeting the aircraft had received, darkness was falling.

So far there had been no sign of anyone appearing to refuel the Swift, so I went over to the duty officer to see if this matter could be expedited. Explaining to the duty officer, I wanted to leave Tatoi at 10 o'clock that night, but could not do so without full fuel tanks, I appealed to him for help, only to be told be had already telephoned the Athens office of the oil company without success. This being Sunday was probably the reason.

In a dilemma, I decided to seek out the Vacuum manager. The duty officer co-operated by phoning for a taxi and instructing the driver - who knew no English - to take me to the British Embassy which seemed to be the best place to commence the search.

Before leaving the aerodrome, I was told there would be no one on duty at 10 o'clock that night, except the guard, so it would be necessary to peg the aircraft down in the lee of a Hangar. I was rather worried about this, but the duty officer assured me, his men knew their job.

I have been frightened many times, but never more than during that drive, at 'breakneck' speed, to Athens. My plea to slow down seemed to spur on the driver, who with one hand on the wheel and the other on the horn button, seemed bent on both manslaughter and suicide.

Arriving in a state of acute nervous tension, I was plunged to the depth of despair by finding the Embassy closed.

By signs I tried to persuade the driver to return to the aerodrome, instead be took me for a tour of the city.

Brilliantly lit shops, trains, motor cars, ancient edifices and pedestrians in large numbers swept by in kaleidoscopic medley.

In a daze, I again implored the driver to return to Tatoi, but I might well have been King Canute and he the tide for all the notice he took.

I was becoming desperate when the taxi was halted by the congested traffic outside a building on which a sign read 'British Chamber of Commerce Club.' In a flash I was out of the taxi, running up a flight of steps leading to the club.

Rushing through the entrance, I almost collided with a fierce looking fellow, who testily demanded in a broad Scottish accent 'What the devil do you mean by barging in here?'

"Thank goodness you can speak English', I ejaculated. 'Where can I find Mr Anderson, the manager of the Vacuum Oil Company please?'

The dour Scott gazed at me suspiciously for a few seconds, then demanded. 'And what would a dirty looking body like you be wanting with Mr Anderson on the Sabbath?'

I explained to the Scot, who proved to be a most kindly person, who I was and why I wanted to locate Anderson, so urgently.

The forthright Scot took another good look at me and said. 'Well! to me you look more like a chimney sweep than an aviator. Mr Anderson is a friend of mine who lives somewhere out Piraeus way, I can't explain where, but I think I can find the place if we can get a cab.'

I came by taxi,' I said. 'But I expect the driver has gone to the police to complain about my clearing out without paying the fare'.

'Don't worry, the fellow will be outside waiting for you, if I know anything about Greek cabbies'. The Scot was right. As soon as he saw me, the driver greeted me with a tirade in Greek, soon silenced by the Scot who directed the driver on another nervewracking journey which ended eventually at the home of Mr Anderson.

Although he had received news of my projected flight, Mr Anderson was astounded by my arrival, before the news of my departure from England or the estimated time of my arrival at Athens.

On learning of my desire to be on my way as soon as possible, Anderson set out immediately for his office in Athens to obtain the keys of the Tatoi fuel depot. Meanwhile Mrs Anderson prepared an excellent meal which I devoured after soaking out my tiredness and dirt in a hot bath.

Seeing my image in the bathroom mirror, I realised the reason why the Scot (I never learned his name) had likened me to a chimney sweep, except for the area around my eyes, which had been protected by goggles, my face was filthy.

I was feeling fresher and fitter than at any time since leaving England, by the time Mr Anderson returned. He had found a telegram pushed under the door of his office, stating I had departed from Lympne at 5am Saturday and was expected to arrive at Athens early on Sunday morning.

The telegram was apparently delivered after the office had closed on Saturday.

It was after 10 oclock when we reached Tatoi and a quarter to eleven by the time the Swift had been refuelled and I was ready to leave. Before getting into the Swift, I put on the carpet slippers given me by my aunt, hoping these would do a better job at keeping out the cold than my shoes.

The wind had backed a little, but it was still an icy gale blowing down out of the mountains from the north.

'A most unpleasant night to go flying,' Mr Anderson remarked when I said goodbye and thanked him for his hospitality.

Except for a solitary light in the guard room, the aerodrome was a black void pierced only by the headlights of Anderson's car. A faint glow on the overcast over Athens was the only other sign of light.

Taking a heavily laden aircraft off the ground without an adequate directional guide could be hazardous in normal circumstances. Any unevenness in the aerodrome surface or wind oscillation could start a swing which might become uncontrollable unless seen and checked immediately. Something I would not have to worry about tonight, once the Swift was facing into the wind. The main problem now would be preventing the aircraft from turning over as it left the lee of the hangar and was turning into wind.

Applying full aileron to keep the windward wing down as much as possible when the aircraft came away from the protection of the hangar, I opened the throttle fully. The Swift moved forward, the tail started to rise. Then the wind struck, the starboard wing started to dip almost striking the ground, as the Swift whipped round into wind. The aircraft skidded a few inches, then shot into the air, dropped back again on to one wheel, finally climbing away into the wind. The shortest takeoff I had ever experienced.

The climb out of Tatoi was like riding a switchback railway. At 1,500 feet, a few lights appeared below, the only outside indication that the Swift was right side up.

I gradually turned the aircraft on course, catching a glimpse of the lights of Athens away on the starboard side, as the Swift came round on track.

A few seconds later the Swift entered cloud, battling with the turbulence as it climbed towards the invisible stars. Minutes later the enveloping cloud cleared disclosing the foam fringed island of Petali, barely visible about a mile away to the north.

Already the aircraft was well south of the track to Aleppo despite the allowance of 25 degrees I had made for drift. Guessing the wind velocity, at this height to be between 80 and 90 miles per hour, I brought the Swift round another 10 degrees to port, a total offset of 35 degrees to the true course.

Although I had taken careful note of the direction and velocity of the surface wind at Tatoi, it was impossible to assess the conditions aloft.

No forecast of the weather between Athens and Aleppo had been available so there was no knowing what the conditions were like enroute.

Had I not - by the grace of God - been given a glimpse of Petali at a propitious moment, there was no knowing where the flight would have ended. Even now that was a matter for conjecture.

The cloud closed in almost immediately after altering course and with the cloud came rain.

Aware the terrain, on some of the islands ahead, reached above the present altitude of the aircraft, I took the machine up to 8,000 feet. At this altitude the Swift with its heavy load felt very sluggish, wallowing in the turbulence, which was, at times, quite violent, making it difficult to maintain altitude.

The turbulence became progressively worse, forcing the aircraft down to below 6,000 feet. The indicated air speed had also dropped instead of increasing at the lower altitude, it was now showing 80 miles per hour, 10 miles per hour less than it should have been indicating.

Although the engine was operating normally, the Swift continued to lose height. Assuming the airspeed reading to be false and the sluggish feeling in the controls a figment of my imagination, I eased the stick back until the airspeed indicator showed 75 miles per hour. Height was maintained for a short while, then the downward trend began again.

Opening the throttle fully, stayed the descent for a minute or so. Despite my efforts the Swift continued to descend until it was below 5,000 feet.

Puzzled and rather frightened, I had visions of suffering a similar fate to that of Icarus, who - reputedly - ended his ill fated flight in the sea only a few leagues away from the spot where the Swift was now being mauled by the elements.

It seemed as if the ancient gods of these parts were bent on destroying those who trespassed on their aerial domains. A ridiculous thought. Yet! some mysterious power was forcing the aircraft down towards the sea.

Whilst my mind was trying to figure out, in a detached sort of way, the cause and remedy for my predicament, my hands - sweating at the palms - and feet wrestled to keep the Swift on even keel.

Although only 40 minutes had elapsed since taking off from Tatoi, I was beginning to feel very fatigued. The turn and bank indicator which was supposed to make blind flying easy, proved useless in these conditions, being far too sensitive for me to follow the rapid oscillations of its two needles.

Down at 4,000 feet, realising the futility of running the engine flat out, I throttled back to normal power.

The descent became more rapid and it looked as if the Swift would soon be in the sea or wrecked on one of the Sporades within the next few minutes, unless a miracle happened.

At 3,400 feet, the Swift ran into a particularly bad stretch of turbulence. The sluggishness disappeared and the aircraft started to gain height as the airspeed built up to 80, then 85 miles per hour. I eased the stick back and the Swift bucked its way heavenward.

Fear of the thing which had thrust the Swift down more than 4,000 feet, before releasing its clutch and the uncertainty of finding Tatoi in the darkness, prevented me from turning back, but I had grave doubts about my ability to cope with the existing conditions if they continued much longer.

At 7,500 feet the Swift refused to go an inch higher, it seemed as if it was aware of the peril lurking above.

Again the controls became sluggish. The thing had us in its grip again, pushing the Swift down and down even lower.

On the verge of panic, I realised the futility of trying to fight against this unknown and unseen adversary and concentrated on trying to keep the Swift's nose pointing somewhere in the direction of Aleppo.

The aircraft ceased to descend when it again reached 3,500 feet or thereabouts. The usual sensitivity of the controls returned and, apart from the continuous buffeting, things seemed normal.

I would have remained at this level had it not been for the risk of ramming the mountains of Ikaria Island, somewhere in the murk ahead. Fear of this caused me to climb to 5,000 feet, where the Swift continued to behave normally, until 80 minutes out from Tatoi, a severe updraught shot the Swift up to well over 6,000 feet. It seemed as if the mysterious menace lurking above was drawing the Swift back into its clutches, when the aircraft was thrust down to 5,000 feet again.

During the following 30 minutes a gradual change for the better took place. The rain squalls were not so frequent and the turbulence less violent, which was just as well because fatigue and fear had almost driven me to the end of my tether.

Although I had endeavoured to keep on course, the Swift had, for most of the time during the past hour, been yawing considerably and could well be far from the track to Aleppo, and would, quite likely, finish up in Asia Minor or, perhaps, in the Holy Land.

A landfall in either one of these places being a possibility if the Swift continued yawing the way it was at present.

When the star first appeared I thought it a figment of my imagination. For a fleeting second it shone, almost overhead before vanishing, to appear several seconds later in company with several less brilliant stars. The cloud above gradually disappeared leaving the heavenly canopy to shed its soft light on a few clouds remaining below.

As the cloud dispersed so did my fatigue and fear. Keeping the Swift on course became easy despite the turbulence which still persisted in flinging the Swift about.

At 11.10pm Greenwich Mean Time on Sunday (1.10am Monday, Greek time) and two hours fifteen minutes after departure, the Swift passed over a small island and a smudge of land appeared away to the left, soon land was also showing over to the right.

Ten minutes later the Swift crossed a foam fringed coast a few miles south of a cluster of lights indicating a town which could be Millasa. If this assumption was correct, the Swift had drifted at least 25 miles to the south of the direct track to Aleppo despite a large offset made to counteract the northerly wind.

Not very happy about the uncertainty of my position, I continued on the present course, anticipating the wind would moderate, thus allowing the Swift to come back towards the direct track. Should the drift persist, the aircraft would eventually reach the Mediterranean coast, where I hoped to recognise some point which would enable me to set a fresh course to Aleppo.

Although I was unable to tell its direction, the wind seemed to be more of a help than a hindrance, judged by the swiftness with which the lights of the town faded astern.

I had studied intensively the two strip maps covering the Athens-Aleppo section of the route, but it was impossible to memorise, in detail, a stretch of over 760 miles. It was also impossible to study a map, by the light of a torch, whilst attempting to control the Swift which was still bucking about in a lively manner.

The cloud had now vanished completely, leaving the sky to the stars which seemed very brilliant in this part of the world.

Soon the horizon ahead was marred by high mountains looming up so suddenly, I was forced to turn back and climb the Swift to 10,000 feet before continuing on course.

During the climb, the waning moon - well towards its last quarter - rose silhouetting the jagged peaks athwart the track.

As the Swift gained altitude, the turbulence eased, but the cold became intense. Despite this, I was feeling so contented and confident, it was hard to believe that less than an hour ago I had been a craven creature on the verge of exhaustion and barely capable of coherent thought.

Such a transition in so short a time puzzled me. It was like awakening in the morning, after suffering a terrible nightmare, relieved that it had only been a dream.

The happening over the Agean Sea had been no dream, it had been an encounter with some mysterious force, so demoralizing it would remain imprinted indelibly on my memory.

During the next 90 minutes, the Swift sped through the calm night air towards the crescent moon whose faint light penetrated the black void below, insufficiently, however, for landmarks to be recognized, but enough for its reflection to be seen on water ahead.

The Gulf of Adalia, I assumed, showing up about the time I had estimated.

My assumption was shattered a minute or so later, when the silhouette of a range of high mountains appeared beyond the glistening water which turned out to be a fairly large lake.

Although it was too dark to distinguish its size and shape, I fished out my torch and conned the map. There were two lakes close together a few miles west of the Gulf of Adalia and another to the north of the Gulf, about on the direct track between Milassa and Aleppo.

Assuming the latter to be the lake just flown over, I continued on course, hoping to reach the Mediterranean coast somewhere near the town of Mesin, within the next two hours.

Forty five minutes later, the glint of water again showed ahead. This was rather disconcerting, because if the Swift was on the track I thought it was, no water should have been sighted before I reached the Mediterranean.

I again consulted the map, without avail. Thousands of square miles of Turkey seemed to be strewn with lakes of all shapes and sizes. Excellent marks for locating position in daylight, but very confusing at night. I hadn't the faintest idea where I was and might well be heading towards Russia instead of Syria.

Two things could have caused this dilemma. Either the compass could have become faulty during the heavy jolting the Swift had received in the storm or there had been a drastic change in the wind.

Picking a star at right angles to the present compass heading, I turned through a 90 degree arc. The compass needle steadied on a bearing correct to within a degree or so and returned to its previous reading when I brought the aircraft back to its original course. There was apparently nothing wrong with the compass. So there must have been a change in the wind. The question was, when and to what degree.

My speculation was interrupted by a sudden slackness of feeling in the fuel pump handle which I had been working intermittently since the Swift had shaken itself clear of the storm.

The auxiliary fuel tank had been pumped dry. The fuel remaining was barely sufficient to sustain the Swift aloft for another three and a half hours.

For better or worse, I decided to bring the Swift round on to the same compass heading as the direct course from Athens to Aleppo. The Swift would now be travelling parallel to the direct track if the air was still; this was most unlikely at the present altitude of 10,000 feet. If the wind was still from the north, the Mediterranean would show up sooner or later, but if the wind had swung to any quarter in the south, only Providence knew what the result would be.

For over an hour the Swift sped over a land of shadows never clearly defined, giving the impression of being sometimes very close, at others as remote as the stars.

Cruising through the perfectly calm atmosphere between the star strewn heavens above and the shadow land below created a feeling of acute loneliness which produced a tranquility of mind, followed eventually by a sense of exultation quite unlike anything I had experienced previously.

At 3.45am G.M.T. the landscape was again sheathed in cloud turned to silver by the pale light cast by the moon now well on its way to its zenith.

That the cloud might extend to Aleppo or beyond, even farther than the ultimate range of the Swift caused me not the slightest concern. In my present mood such a mundane matter seemed of little importance. I felt quite capable of coping with anything short of the disintegration of the aircraft.

Forty five minutes later subtle change came over the scene. The moon and stars seemed to recede and the colour of the clouds below changed to pale cream, rose then to crimson until it appeared as if the unseen Earth below had become an inferno which cast its ruddy glow through the clouds creating a magnificent and awe inspiring spectacle.

Suddenly the colour in the clouds vanished and with it the night, leaving a lone star in the east, soon to be banished by a bloated ruddy sun rising above the clouds, which again changed colour for a few seconds, adding a splendid finale to a dramatic sunrise.

Soon the clouds disappeared revealing a stretch of water bounded by a coast which, after extending a few miles to the northeast, curved round to disappear in the haze to the southeast.

By the grace of God, the Swift had reached the head of the Gulf of Iskenderum, about 20 miles north of the direct track to Aleppo.

I took the Swift down over the gulf to its eastern shore, on over the drab country beyond to touch down on Aleppo aerodrome at exactly 7.30am local time, with less than 3 gallons of fuel remaining in the aircraft.

The longest stage of the journey had been successfully accomplished.

The stony surface of Aleppo aerodrome was very rough, but its deficiencies were more than compensated for, by the French Air Force which gave me a great welcome. There was much enthusiasm about the flight and that the journey from Marseille had been accomplished in the elapsed time of 42 hours. An effort considered worthy enough for a celebration, but drinking champagne before breakfast was not my 'cup of tea'. Feeling elated enough as it was, I settled for a cup of coffee. The best coffee I had ever tasted.

Curbing my impatience to be on my way as soon as the Swift had been refuelled, I made a thorough examination of the aircraft, paying particular attention to the damaged strut and lead, they both appeared to be in satisfactory condition. The engine was in perfect order, but the leading edges of the wings, tail plane and fin had been almost denuded of paint, which had disappeared completely from the leading edges of the propeller blades, fortunately the fabric stockings were not frayed.

A considerable amount of paint had also gone from the front of the engine cowling.

The rigging and controls appeared to be normal, giving no clue to cause of the sluggishness which had occurred twice during the storm over the Agean Sea, leaving me puzzled as to a logical explanation for this phenomenon.

I was perspiring profusely by the time I had removed the canvas muff from the oil cooler which had been fitted to enable the engine to be run for long periods in the torrid conditions which would be experienced from now on.

Although it was wintertime and not yet 10am the temperature had risen to over 33° centigrade (over 90° fahrenheit), causing me to shed most of my clothes before I had finished the job.

Taking the Swift off the ground at Aleppo proved quite hazardous. The wind that had pushed the Swift along so fast over the last hundred miles had dropped to a mere zephyr, this coupled with the high temperature, caused the aircraft to take a much longer run than usual before becoming airborne.

The worst feature, however, was the many large stones strewn about the surface.

Fortunately the undercarriage survived the battering it received and the Swift eventually left the ground within a few yards from the boundary of the aerodrome, climbing slowly to 6,000 feet, where the temperature was quite pleasant. At this altitude the wind was still on my tail, pushing the Swift along so fast, Lake Jabul, 30 miles from Aleppo was reached within 15 minutes.

There was little turbulence and except for a light haze, visibility was good, ideal conditions for a fast and comfortable flight to Basra, where I hoped to arrive before sunset.

Fifteen minutes after passing Lake Jabul, the Euphrates River could be seen away over to the left. Ahead and to the right the drab desert stretched to infinity.

The horizon began to close in gradually as the Euphrates faded from sight to the northeast leaving a treeless terrain devoid of habitation, with not even a watercourse to relieve the monotony. A barren mottled land whose forbidding appearance gave the impression that a landing upon it could be fatal.

Sometime later the Euphrates showed up again and when El Kajim, 260 miles from Aleppo, slid by a few minutes later, it was obvious the wind had changed. The Swift was not only a few miles to the left of its track, it was also making slower time.

By now visibility was less than ten miles and the air was becoming turbulent.

On the few occasions I had encountered dust storms in Australia, their advent had been disconcerting. Extending thousands of feet into the air, the waves of black or red dust advancing across the country made quite a spectacle until it enshrouded everything in a pall so thick, that the sun becomes invisible and the day so dark, lights are necessary.

In the contrast to the rapid and definite approach of Australian dust storms, the sands of Arabia seemed to be materialising out of the air in a sneaky sort of way. A grey, suffocating cloak, which forced me to take the Swift down to about 500 feet from the ground.

It was now difficult to see more than a mile and had it not been for fear of consequences I would have attempted to land. Recollection of stories of atrocities committed by nomads who roamed this desert region and tales about those who had suffered and died from heat exhaustion, compelled me to continue.

Soon the Swift was down to 50 feet, even at this height the ground was indistinct. There seemed to be little wind, but what there was could well have been blowing out of Hades, for the heat, at this level, was almost unbearable, forcing me to climb back to 6,000 feet, where neither the sun nor the ground was visible.

The dim prospect of failing to locate Basra in these conditions before nightfall and the possibility of running out of fuel whilst searching for the place, made me decide to divert to Baghdad and if I could find the place, stay there until conditions improved.

I altered course at 10.55am G.M.T. - when by my reckoning Baghdad was approximately 165 miles away - and allowed 10° for drift on the assumption that the wind direction was the same as on the ground with its velocity a few miles greater.

I was not very happy about this guesswork, not that it was vital to fly a direct course to Baghdad, a few degrees off course in either direction would not matter. It was essential, however, to make sure the Swift didn't overshoot the Tigris River and end up in the mountainous wilderness of Persia.

Becoming sick of ploughing along, half suffocated and in semi darkness, I tried to climb out of the murk. At 10,000 feet the dust was sparse enough for the rays of the sun to penetrate and the feeling of claustrophobia, from which I was beginning to suffer, disappeared, so I kept to this altitude.

With nothing to do but keep the compass needle aligned to the grid, my thoughts turned to the lady, which brought to mind that I was not far from the spot where the first man in biblical history was supposed to have plighted his troth. I wondered how many millions of tons, of what was once the Garden of Eden, had been whisked up into the surrounding atmosphere, and where it had been finally deposited.

It must have been a fertile spot, once upon a time. At least fertile enough to produce an apple tree.

My mind meandered through what I read of biblical history, whilst my eyes kept careful watch on the instruments, until the time came to descend.

Seventy minutes had passed since changing course, and if my navigation had been correct, Baghdad was less than 50 miles away.

Before descending, I made a careful perusal of the map, memorising details in the vicinity of Baghdad, because it would be impossible to refer to the map should the visibility compel me to fly close to the ground on the final stage.

I pushed the Swift down at about 500 feet per minute until the altimeter showed 1,000 feet. The instrument had been set at zero before leaving Aleppo, which was approximately 1,300 feet above sea level. The Tigris Valley was lower than this, but not knowing by how much, I eased the rate of descent. Throttling the engine back and allowing the Swift - almost stalled - to sink in a more or less horizontal attitude so that if the ground appeared too suddenly for me to prevent contact, the aircraft would bounce instead of flying into the ground.

To hold the aircraft in this somewhat precarious attitude, I soon found it necessary to increase engine power. By the time the altimeter was showing zero, I had been able to adjust the rate of descent, so that it could not have been more than 100 feet per minute. Of course, all this was guesswork. It was impossible to calculate a rate of descent by comparing the movement of the altimeter needle with the elapse of time shown on the clock and fly the machine as well.

It was difficult enough to keep the Swift on a steady heading, in this altitude and under proper control, without sight of the horizon or the ground. Fortunately the false mental impulse which had caused me so much stress, on my first 'blind' flight, no longer bothered me.

When the Swift had descended to minus 500 feet (about 800 feet above sea level), l poked my head out of the cockpit, scanning the murk below for a sight of the Earth.

Shortly after, a slight shudder in the elevator control gave warning that the Swift was on the verge of stalling, causing me to ram the throttle wide open and ease the stick forward.

As the aircraft gathered speed, the ground suddenly appeared about 15 to 20 feet below, with the gap closing so rapidly, it was only by a narrow margin contact was avoided as I levelled out and adjusted the throttle to maintain a speed of 75 miles per hour.

The sand seemed to be moving in waves, with visibility varying from 400 yards down to no more than 50 feet, but it was seldom possible to see more than 200 feet.

Like most pilots, I rather enjoyed a bit of 'contour chasing', on a clear calm day. It is thrilling to have the ground slipping by a few feet below and to feel the response of the aircraft as it is skipped over a telegraph line or a tree.

Without doubt, the contour chasing in which I was now engaged was thrilling, but anticipation of some unsurmountable obstacle appearing suddenly ahead was far from enjoyable.

An additional anxiety was the possibility of failing to locate Baghdad aerodrome, situated somewhere south of the city, which should, by now, be less than twenty miles away.

To obtain a clearer view ahead, I crabbed the Swift along by using a little right rudder, counteracting the tendency to turn by applying slight left aileron.

The Swift plowed through the dust for what seemed an indeterminable time without any change of scene, then I caught a fleeting glimpse of a startled Arab sheltering in the lee of a kneeling camel, as the Swift sped by a few feet above their heads.

A few minutes later I began to have grave misgivings about my whereabouts. By my reckoning the Swift should have reached Baghdad by now, if not Baghdad, then the Tigris River which lay athwart my course.

Although it would have been well nigh impossible to have flown beyond Baghdad or to have crossed the Tigris whilst the Swift was descending through the dust, the idea that this might have occurred, tempted me to turn back.

In circumstances like this, it is not easy to keep check of time and distance, when intense concentration is required to keep the aircraft on course, avoid flying into the ground and also be on the alert to take evasive action should an obstacle appear suddenly ahead.

Resisting temptation, I continued on my way.

Minutes later, a few bushes flashed by a few inches below the wheels, then trees appeared suddenly out of the dust. I rammed the throttle open and pulled back the stick. The Swift shot up like a rocket, missing the palms by a very small margin.

For a fleeting second I thought I saw water beyond, then the dust obscured everything as the Swift climbed skyward. Throttling back I eased the Swift into a left hand gliding turn. As height was lost, the tops of palms appeared indistinctly beneath, then visibility improved slightly, revealing on my left, a river, heading north and south.

Remembering the Tigris ran in a southerly direction above Baghdad, where it turned to the south east, I made a shallow 180° turn, conscious of the close proximity of the palms below.

By the time the turn had been completed and the Swift was heading south, the river had vanished somewhere on my left. As I eased the aircraft round to find it, visibility improved slightly revealing a few buildings, a few trees and then more buildings extending into the pall of dust.

By the grace of God, the Swift had arrived over Baghdad, all that I had to do now was find the aerodrome.

After narrowly avoiding the wrath of the followers of Mohammed by dodging a couple of minarets more by luck than skill, I eventually reached the area where the aerodrome should be.

In vain I searched for signs of a hangar, windsock or a circle, in fact anything that would give me a clue, but the dust was too thick to see anything at this height and I was afraid to go lower, it was too much of a risk.

After flying around for what seemed an eternity, the dust cleared sufficiently to show a spot of clear ground almost beneath the aircraft. Cutting the engine, I sideslipped the Swift almost to ground level, where the way ahead was clear for about 100 feet. Thoroughly alarmed by my plight, I put the aircraft down, praying that there were no obstructions in the way.

The aircraft rolled to a stop over smooth ground. I sat trying to gather my wits, conscious only of the faint sounds caused by the contraction of the engine.

I was still sitting in the machine when a giant of a man loomed out of the dust. Without preamble, he demanded. 'Have you been inoculated?' The fellow was no Arab, nor English either by the way he spoke.

He wasn't concerned about my papers, from whence I had come or whither I was bound, nor that I was half dead from fatigue, fear and thirst. No! All that concerned him - Had I been inoculated.

Speechless, I gazed at this man, who continued. 'Quickly! Let me see your health certificate'.

Puzzled by this strange encounter on a sand blasted desert, I meekly 'fished out' the letter the Hythe doctor had given me. My interrogator examined the certificate, while I undid my harness and heaved myself out of the cockpit.

Hurriedly the man thrust the certificate back to me saying as he did so. 'Don't forget to say you had two jabs before leaving, if they ask any questions.'

More puzzled than ever, I demanded 'Look here! What is going on. Who are they and who are you and, by the way, where am I?'

My erstwhile interrogator grinned 'You can't kid me you don't know this is Baghdad. Maloney is my name and be thankful I got to you first', he replied, as another figure loomed out of the dust which was now so thick, it was impossible to see more than a few feet.

The new arrival was a Government official, who with the help of Maloney guided me - not without difficulty - to the tarmac.

Accompanied by Maloney, I was taken to an office where the police examined my papers, paying particular attention to my medical certificate. My passport was stamped and I was told to go, without one question being asked.

Maloney then escorted me over to his quarters, telling me on the way, that he was Imperial Airways Baghdad representative, also that he and his staff had been following my flight with great interest. When they heard of my departure from Aleppo for Basra, they expected I would have enough 'gumption' to make for Baghdad, if I ran into the sandstorm.

Still curious about the way he had greeted me on arrival, I asked Maloney why the concern about my health certificate. 'Well' he said, 'there is a cholera epidemic in Baghdad, and if you hadn't been inoculated, the local wallahs would have 'bunged' you into quarantine for a couple of weeks and done the jabbing' themselves'.

I told him I hadn't been inoculated and asked if I should be if there was a possibility of my catching cholera. The idea of contracting this disease rather alarmed me.

'Don't worry, you won't have the chance, I'll not be letting you out of my sight until you take off for Basra. You've got that midge of yours this far and you've got to keep going to crack the record of that English spalpeen Scott. My money is on you, so you're staying right here on this aerodrome with me.' The big man with the lush brogue grinned.

Still puzzled, I asked why the police had cleared me without inquiring if I had been immunized. The big Irishman ignored my question by saying 'I think the sand will clear by morning, we'll get you away as soon as it does, so you had better have something to eat and get your head down for a few hours.

I was asleep within an hour, and after what seemed seconds being awakened by my friend who informed me that it was 2am, the sky was clear and it was time 'I got cracking'.

When I pointed out, that leaving before 3.30am would mean arriving in Basra before dawn, Maloney said 'Don't worry about that, I've contacted our boys. If you get to Basra before daylight they will light flares for you, but I think you will strike a headwind up top which will slow you down a lot.'

Arabia is a place of strange contrasts. I had arrived at Baghdad in torrid heat, although it was late Autumn, and despite the sun being obscured by dust. Now, a few hours later, the cold was intense and the sky so clear it was hard to believe it had ever been sullied by even so much as a speck of dust. The thin crescent of the moon, just arisen and the stars shed their soft light on a still and silent world.

In most places it is surprising the amount of noise usually heard throughout the hours of darkness, but in this place, adjacent to a city of at least a quarter of a million, the silence was not only exceptional, it was uncanny. No rustle of leaves, ripple of water, nor the noise of any animal or vehicle disturbed the still air. Not even the cry of a night bird.

Here, at this hour, the silence was absolute if one held one's breath. It did not remain that way for long. The engine started first pull, its staccato exhaust shattering the silence.

Although glad to be leaving this pest ridden spot, I was sorry, in a way, to say farewell to my cheerful Irish friend, who had looked after me like a hen with one chick.

There was no wind and no flares to aid my takeoff, but by sighting a bright star ahead, I was able to keep the Swift straight during its pre-takeoff run.

Becoming airborne at 2.50am local time, I took the Swift up to 10,000 feet - where the exhaust would be invisible from the ground - mindful of the fate of Cobham's engineer, Elliot who, on a flight between Baghdad and Basra, had been fatally shot from the ground by an Arab.

It was bitterly cold at this altitude, almost too cold to think, all the same, it did not prevent me from puzzling over my stay at Baghdad.

On arrival, being too tired to think clearly, I had accepted things as they came. Now, I could not help wondering about the events which had occurred. Maloney's unusual concern about my health certificate and advice to tell the authorities, should they question me, that I had been twice inoculated. Yet! the aerodrome officials, when examining my papers, had made no comment. In fact Maloney had been the only one to mention cholera. Perhaps he had a phobia about the disease.

The alleged epidemic could be a figment of his imagination, although Maloney seemed to be a very stable sort of person despite his insistence that I should wash in and drink only boiled water, also his care about the food I had been allowed to eat whilst being his guest.

The matter was still occupying my mind when the first flash of dawn showed in the east. Daylight came quickly revealing a mist which hung gossamer-like above the landscape. A few minutes later the Swift was over Basra, its buildings showing faintly through the mist which reduced visibility to zero when the Swift entered it. Then the engine cut out, causing me a few anxious seconds, until the aircraft glided clear of the evil smelling murk, about 50 feet above the ground. Once clear of the mist the engine came to life again, almost causing me to overshoot the aerodrome.

The cause of the engine failure became evident when I tested the ignition. The rear bank of plugs had failed and when the Swift had entered the mist, the filthy smelling stuff had shorted the front bank thus depriving the engine of ignition.

It did not take long for British Imperial Airways engineers to locate the trouble, the damaged lead had failed again. In less than an hour a completely new lead had been made and fitted, smart work so early in the morning.

Meanwhile the local authorities examined my papers, then asked where I had spent the night at Baghdad, they seemed quite relieved when I told them I had not been away from the aerodrome.

My papers were returned and I was taken over to Imperial Airways mess for breakfast, here I was questioned about the concern in England regarding the cholera epidemic raging in the Baghdad area. Everyone present was surprised to learn that, to my knowledge, nothing was known about the matter in Britain.

Someone said 'All the local authorities have the 'wind up' about the epidemic which is so serious, the Lord only knows what will happen if it isn't contained.'

By the time I had finished breakfast, work on the Swift had been completed, the aircraft had been refuelled and an engineer was standing by to swing the propeller.

My offer, to pay for the repairs, was refused and I was advised to get away as soon as possible.

The Swift shook the dust of Basra from its wheels at 7.25am local time, exactly one hour after my arrival. Forty minutes later it was at 6,000 feet over the Persian Gulf, where the temperature was at least 50° higher than it had been at this altitude less than two hours ago.

Although the sun had arisen little more than half an hour before my departure, the temperature at Basra was well on the way to the century mark. A great contrast to the winter climate at Coffs Harbour which is on the same latitude.

Within an hour the land had disappeared fading away to the north. The Swift was again encompassed by two dishes of blue, azure above, paler and mottled by shadows below, with neither the air nor the sea disturbed by the slightest ripple. Conditions similar to those over the Ligurian Sea, but here there was no feeling of claustrophobia. Perhaps I was becoming inured to this sort of thing.

Eventually, Kharag Island appeared about 5 miles away to the port. Twenty minutes later the Swift was opposite Bushure, with the coast of Persia rapidly taking shape ahead.

On this stage the Swift had, so far, averaged slightly over 100 miles per hour. The head wind I encountered on the Baghdad-Basra stage had apparently disappeared.

Persia, turned out to be a very disappointing landscape, mountainous and barren. For hours the Swift sped over this forbidding, desolate country, which eventually gave way to the salt marches of Mihrakan.

The Swift had been in the air for five hours when I sighted Linjah on the Gulf of Ormuz, on the far side of which the Oman Peninsula was clearly defined.

Although more than eighty miles away, the rugged peninsula appeared to be less than half that distance, so clear was the atmosphere.

Fifteen minutes later and twenty miles closer, the peninsula seemed no nearer, in fact, it appeared to be receding, giving the impression it was falling away over the edge of the earth. This may have been caused by some peculiarity in the atmosphere - a mirage perhaps - or it may have been imagination on my part.

A few minutes later, this awe inspiring Arabian massif, its huge bulk thrusting the waters of the gulf up into the belly of Persia, seemed to be advancing with a rapidity that appeared quite menacing.

This great hunk of rock, rearing sheer from the sea over 6,000 feet below, the mightiest cliff I had ever seen, caused a brief feeling of vertigo when I glanced over the side as the aircraft passed over, a few hundred feet above the edge of the precipice.

The top formed a tableland, broken by ravines, falling away to the north until, in the far distance, it ended in the gulf.

Despite the isolated, rugged terrain, there were signs of civilisation, and parts of the land appeared suitable for grazing, but no water was visible, or any roads, not even a goat track.

It took the Swift 15 minutes to cross Oman and I was quite happy to see the last of Arabia, its mountains, sand, smells and its pestilence.

Once clear of the mountains, I started to descend gradually over the eastern arm of the Gulf of Omuz, heading for Jask, 100 miles away.

The Swift touched down 55 minutes later on a vast sunbaked plain, east of the town. The largest aerodrome I had so far seen.

Although the flight from Basra had only averaged 99 miles per hour, conditions had been so good I was tempted to fly on to Karachi immediately after refuelling, but thoughts of my narrow escape at Naples caused me to defer takeoff to allow for arrival at Karachi, at daybreak. There was too much at stake to take any more foolish risks.

As I taxied towards the buildings, I noticed a truck, containing several men armed with rifles, racing alongside the aircraft. One of the occupants, alongside the driver, was waving his arms and shouting either a welcome or a warning. The combined noise of the aircraft and the vehicle precluded me from hearing what the performance was about.

Nearing the buildings the truck was accelerated and driven in front of the Swift. Switching off the engine immediately, I swung the aircraft round to avoid a collision.

As the port wing swept round and over the top of the rear of the truck, only the alacrity of the soldiers in jumping clear, prevented them from being skittled.

I jumped out of the cockpit quickly, intending to give the driver 'a piece of my mind'. Two of the soldiers were just as quick. Before I had taken two paces towards the truck, they were covering me with their rifles.

Thoroughly bewildered and rather frightened, I froze in my tracks. Then the person who had been waving and shouting came to within twenty feet of me and in very poor English, warned me to stay away from him - he seemed as scared of me, as I was of his armed companions - because I was a cholera contact and must leave Jask as soon as possible, also I must stay by my aeroplane until I departed. He concluded by telling me if I went near anyone on the aerodrome I would be placed in isolated custody.

He was then driven away, leaving two soldiers, who remained watching me at a safe distance.

Later a young man accompanied by an armed guard, brought fuel and oil for the Swift. He was taken away immediately refuelling had been completed.

By this time the shades of night were falling rapidly and I was beginning to feel rather empty and very thirsty, with the idea of sampling another of my emergency tablets and taking a 'swig' of water from the emergency tank, one of the Imperial Airways staff brought a hurricane lamp, placing it about 20 feet from the aircraft. He apologised for being unsociable, saying that he and his colleagues had been ordered to keep away from me, with the threat of being thrown into the local gaol if there was any disobedience. I was told that the boy who had done the refuelling had been placed in isolation for a couple of weeks because the local authorities were in a real 'flap' over the cholera epidemic in Mesopotamia.

Whilst he was telling me this news, another Imperial Airways man brought me some food and a jug of excellent coffee, which I rapidly consumed before the envious gaze of my guards, who looked as if they would have forgotten their orders, had I invited them to share my meal.

With the coming of night, the temperature fell rapidly. To keep warm I walked round and round the Swift like a tethered goat, hounded by the guards, who would not allow me to stray more than a few yards from the aircraft.

My thoughts centred on the cause of my present isolation and on the mystery of why I had been cleared at Baghdad and Basra without question.

I had hitherto paid scant attention to the health certificate which I had obtained after the cursory medical examination in the inn, at Hythe. I recalled the doctor refusing payment as he wished me luck, also James Jeffs stamping the letter and his comments as he did so.

Had it not been for Jeffs advice. I would now be languishing in quarantine in Mesopotamia.

Going over to the hurricane lamp. I carefully examined the health certificate. There was certainly no record of my being inoculated for cholera. Folding the letter to replace it in its envelope, I was surprised to see written on the back

'First dose 17th October.
Second dose 22nd
October. J.B.C.'

This could well be the reason for my puzzlement and my freedom. I had certainly not been 'dosed' on the days mentioned. In fact prior to the 29th October, the date when the certificate was issued, I had never met Doctor Connor. Also the writing on the back was quite different from that of the doctor.

Other than the Government officials at the various places en route, Maloney was the only person who had seen the document, even so, it had been in his possession for only a minute or so. Yet, it might have been possible for my Irish friend to have taken the law into his hands.

Discovery that my bill of health was not all it should be was rather disconcerting. Knowing nothing about this disease which was causing so much concern hereabouts, I wondered if I might have become infected, not having been immunized, or a carrier, menacing all with whom I came in contact. A terrible thought which impelled me to start walking towards the aerodrome buildings, with the intention of explaining matters to the local authorities.

My guards had other ideas. They hounded me back to the Swift, indicating, by gestures, they would shoot me if I disobeyed.

That meant that my explanation would have to be deferred until I reached Karachi. At least the quarantine quarters in that city would be more comfortable than in this desolate place.

The decrease in temperature was becoming most uncomfortable, so I commenced trotting round the Swift, trailed by the grumbling guards, who, well nigh exhausted, flopped down by the lamp, as soon as I ceased my exercise.

They were a pair of dirty ragamuffins, with shabby uniforms and ancient looking rifles.

As the cold increased, I repeated my gyrations around the Swift. This time, however the guards were content to be spectators.

I would have given much more than a penny for their thoughts as they gazed and grinned as I passed through the circle of light close to where they were huddled. They were probably Moslems and as such, had by now, assumed I had been afflicted by Allah with insanity.

Warmed by my last bout of exercise, I got into the cockpit, hoping to snatch some sleep during the 3 hours remaining before my intended departure, but the cramped cockpit and the penetrating cold soon forced me to resume my trotting.

The minutes dragged by until it was time to go. Before starting the engine, I sprinted about 200 yards in the direction I intended to takeoff, making sure there were no straying goats or other obstacles in the way. Keeping a straight track by sighting a large star well up in the eastern sky.

This unexpected expedition into the wilderness, quite alarmed the guards, who, with loud cries came after me.

They were rather nonplussed when they almost collided with me, as I walked back towards the Swift, peering at the ground on either side. It may have been easier to have made the examination had I taken the lantern, but apart from the fact that it would have been too much to have expected the guards to have had allowed this, it would have been difficult without the aid of light to guide me, to walk directly along the line of intended takeoff.

The guards closed in behind me, and no doubt intrigued by what I was doing, followed suit (curiosity overcoming their fear of close contact with me), although I am sure they had no idea why I was surveying the ground.

Reaching the Swift I lifted its tail and carried it round until the nose was facing the star selected to orient the takeoff. The engine started first kick and by the time I had donned my cap and goggles and fastened the harness, the clock on the dash showed 7.30 Greenwich Mean Time (11pm local time).

A push on the throttle and the Swift roared off into the night sky, heading towards the star in the east, my spirits rising with every foot the Swift gained in altitude.

Immediately they leave the earth, those who venture aloft enter the realm of the unpredictable, the haunt of powerful and capricious elements, where aerial journeying can be most uncomfortable. When the aircraft without warning can be tossed heavenward, or dropped over an invisible precipice towards the earth below.

Sometimes the way is strewn with windy hummocks which jolt the aircraft in a most distressing manner and sometimes storm clouds lie athwart the track to menace those who penetrate their misty masses.

When the elements are dormant, as they are occasionally, one appears to be suspended, motionless in a clear calm sky, whilst the sunlit earth moves by sedately, before the eye, or when night comes to enshroud the land, heaven displays its galaxies which spread soft light upon the scene. It is then flying becomes an exquisite delight.

Such conditions had prevailed since leaving Baghdad over a thousand miles astern, conditions which seemed likely to continue from now on.

Ideal though these conditions were for lulling one to sleep, I had never felt more alert, at this moment although without sleep for over 21 hours.

Intoxicated by the enchantment of this glorious night, I felt akin to those legendary Persians, who roamed the sky on their magic carpets, viewing the marvellous universe with its constellations above the mundane world below, wonderful despite its grubby earthbound creatures, its pestilence, poverty and politics.

Cruising along under the stars, which shone like lanterns in the sky, so brilliant and seemingly so close that one had only to reach up to touch them. My thoughts turned again to Omar Khayam and his attraction to astronomy. What wonderful lines this Persian poet would have written, had he been privileged to ride a wonderful winged chariot like mine.

This mechanical Pegasus carrying me across the world with effortless speed, sweeping through the heavens towards the dawn. Propelled by an engine whose voice rent the air with its unfaltering roar, challenging the Royal Air Force motto *'Per ardua ad astra'*.

With the coming of dawn my exultation vanished like the mist before the sun on a new born day. At daybreak the black void below became a pearly haze, hiding all beneath it. I pushed the Swift down, eager for my first sight of India.

Down at 3,000 feet the sea appeared, curtained by the haze which reduced visibility to about ten miles. My disappointment at not sighting land vanished a few minutes later when the hazy outline of Cape Monae appeared.

The sun rose just as the Swift touched down at Karachi, but its heat was tempered by a fragrant breeze blowing from the east.

Although it was barely 6.30am, a great welcome awaited me when I climbed out of the cockpit to be told the Swift had completed the journey from Great Britain in the fastest time ever. This news gave me little satisfaction because it was much slower than I had planned.

The eastern terminus of Imperial Airways, Karachi, had an excellent aerodrome with imposing buildings dominated by a huge airship hangar which had been built at the time Britain planned to operate its long distance air services with dirigibles.

Although without sleep for more than 26 hours, I needed a bath more than a bed. My last bath and shave had been in Athens, since then my ablutions had been rather sketchy, a hurried wash at Aleppo, a 'cat lick' in boiled water at Baghdad and another hurried wash at Basra, left much to be desired so far as hygiene was concerned.

This was soon remedied by Commander Watt, who was in charge of Karachi Airport.

After a hot bath and excellent breakfast, during which I gave Commander Watt and his charming wife the latest news from England, I broached the subject uppermost on my mind, by asking Commander Watt if, as the result of my sojourn at Baghdad, I could have become a cholera carrier.

'I don't think so', my host replied. 'Unless you have been in contact with someone who has recently suffered or was suffering from the disease, also you would be liable to contract the disease from taking contaminated food and water, unless you have been immunized.'

'I haven't been immunized', I confessed. 'But I drank nothing except boiled water and tea, and everything I ate at Baghdad came out of a tin. The local Imperial Airways manager saw to that'.

'Well you have nothing to worry about' was the reply.

I took off from Karachi, exactly 90 minutes after my arrival, thankful to get away from the ground, which was already becoming unpleasantly hot, although it was barely 8 o'clock.

Soon the Swift was high over the Indus, a noble stream (not unlike a mighty edition of the Murrumbidgee) flowing through the plains of Sind, similar country to the Riverina, between Hay and Narrandera. An attractive scene which soon gave way to the arid Thar desert, a reminder of 'back of Bourke' during a drought.

Fearing the easterly wind would increase with height, I levelled out the Swift at 3,000 feet after climbing out from Karachi. At this height, however, the heat soon became so uncomfortable, I took the Swift up to 9,500 feet where the temperature was reasonably cool.

After flying for more than an hour across the featureless desert, a watercourse, the Luni showed up to break the monotony. A check of time and distance covered since climbing to the present altitude, showed the wind was on my tail. Although it was not strong enough to push the Swift to Allahabad nonstop, calling in at Jhansi to refuel should not prevent me from reaching Allahabad well before sundown.

About noon, the undulating outline of the Aravalli mountains showed on the horizon. Ahead, and far below, deep green vegetation had replaced the drab desert.

As the Swift sped on over this vast and ancient land with its multitude of people, so diversified in race, culture and religion, I wondered about the ultimate fate of the country with its vast potential.

Would religious, social and political enlightenment weld the many races and creeds into a nation able to develop its own resources? Or would the inhabitants be content to remain forever under foreign rule.

Gradually my train of thought on this matter became muddled. The noise of the engine seemed to fade and the wings of the Swift commenced to tilt. With a start I realised I was on the verge of slumber. In desperation I slapped my face, which brought me back to wakefulness. Whilst doing this I was annoyed to discover I had forgotten to shave at Karachi. A worrying omission soon forgotten in my fight to keep awake. Seeing the bar of chocolate, my aunt had given me, which I had tucked behind a fuselage strut before leaving Athens, I decided to sample it, hoping it might stave off the torpidity. Unfortunately the heat had melted the confection which had trickled down to the floor.

Soon the need for sleep became so demanding, I decided to land and rest for a while. With bleary eyes I scanned the terrain for a place to land, but as far as the eye could reach, the country was clothed in thick jungle. Thought of making a landing in such a place drove away the desire for sleep for a short while. Later I must have dozed for a few seconds or minutes, maybe, awaking to find the Swift in a steep sideslip. Thoroughly alarmed I righted the aircraft which had lost over 2,000 feet in altitude.

Fear kept me alert for a brief period, but my lassitude soon returned. In desperation I rubbed my whiskers with my fist, an effective, though painful remedy, which I applied frequently, until after what seemed an eternity, the town of Jhansi showed ahead. A few minutes later the Swift was skimming the long grass of the only paddock of any size in the area.

Two local lads, who brought fuel from the town in a bullock cart, had refuelled the aircraft within 15 minutes of my arrival, leaving plenty of time for me to reach Allahabad before nightfall. Unfortunately I felt incapable of swinging the propeller to start the engine, let alone flying for another two hours.

The heat and high humidity made breathing difficult and accentuated my fatigue, but having no sleep for over 35 hours was the real cause of my exhaustion.

A number of cars arrived, disgorging a number of curious people, one of whom asked me if I would care for a drink and then looked embarrassed when I said I would like some tea.

Although the paddock seemed to be in the middle of nowhere a cup of tea was soon produced. The hot, black, unsweetened and astringent fluid revived me to the extent my brain began to function again.

An ancient bewhiskered Indian appointed himself guardian of the Swift, and some kind person took me into Jhansi. The breeze created by the car helped revive me so that by the time we reached the town, I could at least think coherently again.

I was deposited at an inn, where an elderly Indian woman, in charge of the office, showed her disdain when she instructed a small boy to take me to a room.

After the warm welcome I had received at Karachi, this frigid reception was puzzling until I saw myself in a mirror.

At Athens, I had been likened to a sweep. Had the Scot, who made that comment, seen me now, it is doubtful if even the word 'hobo' would have met his description. My begrimed, bewhiskered face, red raw except where protected by goggles, my bloodshot eyes and untidy hair was most repulsive. My sweat stained shirt and oil stained trousers completed a most unprepossessing picture.

Too tired to care, I kicked off my shoes and flopped on the bed. But sleep was denied me, tired though I was. The noise of the Pobjoy engine echoed in my brain, as I lay in the lather of perspiration, watching the lengthening shadows of the setting sun.

Night came eventually, bringing with it a slightly cooler temperature, yet sleep still eluded me.

This inability to sleep worried me. Although my mind was now functioning clearly, my body ached with fatigue. My shoulders were still raw from the chafing they had received from the harness during the turbulent weather between Brindisi and Aleppo and my buttocks were aching from sitting immobile in a cramped position for such lengthy periods.

Not that these inconveniences mattered so much. There was every likelihood the good weather would continue, at least as far as Singapore.

In fine weather, little or no physical energy was required to fly the Swift.

My main worry was to withstand the mental strain, and I considered the idea of resting at Jhansi for a day rather than risk falling asleep at the controls, which seemed likely to happen again if I continued in my present condition.

My thoughts were interrupted by people conversing in the courtyard adjacent to my room. Conversation which became increasingly louder. Curiosity impelled me to get out of the bed and peep through the bead curtains.

A number of British army officers and their ladies, dressed in their best, were holding a soiree. This scene reminded me of a Strauss operetta, except that it lacked melody.

The place became quiet after a while, so I had the wash I should have had when I arrived, got into my pyjamas and returned to bed, hoping for a few hours sleep.

Eventually, I lapsed into a comatose state bordering slumber, only to be disturbed by a young man entering my room. Before I could demand an explanation for this intrusion, the young man said he had come to take me to Mr Abbot, who wished to see me immediately.

When I demanded to know who Mr Abbot was, the intruder replied, 'My father.'

I brusquely declined the request, it was more like a command than an invitation, but the young man insisted, he seemed rather agitated by my refusal, giving the impression it was a matter of life or death to him. I told him to go away, that I was too tired to get dressed.

Again he implored me to do as he asked, concluding by saying it would be quite in order to pay my respects in my pyjamas.

Too tired to argue further and wondering what sort of tyrant this man's father might be, I donned my carpet slippers and was taken to a mansion nearby.

Never before had I been in such a magnificent home or one with such resplendent furnishings. A palace dominated by the personality of its owner, a very old man who behaved as if he owned the Empire.

With feet ensconced in a tiger skin, I answered the questions put to me by the 'Pukka Sahib', who interrogated me about my aircraft, my flight and myself. Then as soon as his curiosity had been satisfied, my host commanded me to go. To him I was 'less than the dust beneath his chariot wheel'.

I was taken back to the inn, rather puzzled by my experience. By now, it was nearly midnight, and although my body still ached, my mind was too alert for sleep. Instead of going back to bed, I brought my log books up to date.

The Swift had travelled 5,169 miles from England (74 miles beyond the half way point to Australia) in 54 hours 10 minutes flying time and an elapsed time of 4 days 16 hours and 25 minutes.

Although it would be impossible to reach Tooraweenah in the nine days originally intended, it might be possible to do so within ten days, providing the rate of progress during the last two days could be maintained. This meant leaving Jhansi as soon as possible.

Before leaving, I attempted to shave off my beard, a bloody and painful operation, which took nearly an hour, by the time I had staunched the bleeding.

Although it was only a few minutes past one, everyone at the inn had retired, so I set out through the town to search for a vehicle to take me to the aerodrome. Except for the clatter of a shunting train in the distance and a few yapping dogs, Jhansi seemed deserted.

Unfortunately, on my arrival I had been too dazed to arrange for transport to the landing place or to even think about when I intended to depart, so that, now, I had either to wait until the townsfolk started to bestir themselves or set out for the Swift on foot.

Feeling rather depressed about departing like a thief in the night, leaving behind a badly bloodstained towel, which might give the impression that something disastrous had happened, I packed my bag and started off in the direction of where I thought the Swift might be.

Although paying no attention to the direction taken when being driven to Jhansi, I had noted the position of the paddock in relation to the town when I had flown over Jhansi on the way in to land, but it is not always easy to locate a place with only a fleeting glimpse from the air.

After wandering about the countryside for a considerable time I was fortunate to locate the aircraft eventually.

Its guardian protested volubly when I removed the cockpit cover. However with the aid of the torch I was able to satisfy him concerning my bona fides, eventually taking off a few minutes after 3.30am (local time).

As the Swift climbed through the hot humid air, my feeling of depression disappeared, but the joy experienced flying the previous night was absent. The sky was clear, but unlike last night the stars seemed remote.

The atmosphere, also, had a different feel. Here the warm and clammy air seemed to caress one, in an oily sort of way, whereas on the previous night, there was an exhilarating sting about it.

The Swift covered the distance to Allahabad in less than two hours. Passing over Benares half an hour later as the first streaks of dawn appeared.

With a ground speed of more than 120 miles per hour, the Swift was making excellent progress and should arrive in Calcutta about 9am local time and so to Rangoon before sunset that night.

The coming of day revealed a most unusual sight. The countryside dotted with dozens of isolated white balls, scattered about as far as the eye could see.

On descending to investigate this strange phenomenon, which from about 8,000 feet, appeared to be huge balls of cotton wool. I found the objects were spheres of dense cloud of various sizes, ranging, may be, from 100 to 300 feet in diameter, rolling along the ground at about ten miles per hour.

Half an hour later the weather commenced to deteriorate. The isolated clouds, still rolling over the ground below, were closer together and some of them were ragged.

High stratus cloud had drifted in from the south west, obscuring the sun and indicating that more than tea was brewing ahead.

The rain came a couple of miles beyond Gaya, a torrential downpour which forced me to descend to 500 feet. Even at this level visibility was no more than half a mile.

Very soon the rain became such a deluge it was impossible to see more than the length of a football field ahead. To make matters worse, the plains, over which the Swift had flown since daybreak, gave way to undulating country, with scattered timber creating a hazard for the low flying aircraft, which I had taken down to less than 100 feet to see where I was going.

Several near misses caused me to turn back to Gaya, where I hoped to discover the extent of the bad weather.

Before the 180° turn had been completed, the Swift crossed a railway line running in the direction of Calcutta.

To follow a well defined track was a far different matter to barging along over country without sight or knowledge of what may lie ahead, so swinging the Swift round, I headed along the railway, hoping to run out of the rain within a few miles.

From what I had read and heard, the weather in this part of the world followed a fairly regular pattern. Between April and October, the country was under the influence of the south west monsoon which deluged the area with heavy rain and from October to April, the north east monsoon held sway, with fine, calm weather prevailing during the periods of change in the spring and autumn. With this in mind I assumed the present rainstorm to be a local disturbance.

Flying about 20 feet above the rails, I had little difficulty in following the line until it ran into hilly country, where the ever increasing curves made things awkward.

Had the Swift been less maneuverable, the task would have been impossible, as it was, it was necessary to throttle back to the slowest speed safety would permit, to follow the winding track.

Fearing to take my eyes away from the railway even for an instant, in case it vanished, I was unable to look at the instruments, so I had no idea of the time or the distance covered since passing Gaya, nor the altitude of the Swift above sea level, but it was evident the country was becoming more rugged and getting progressively higher.

Embankments and cuttings became more frequent and were higher and deeper. The sides of some of the cuttings rising well above the Swift, not that this was of much concern. There was adequate room for the aircraft, with its small wing span, although I did have difficulty following the line round some of the sharper curves.

Fortunately, the air was calm, otherwise it would have been impossible to have kept so low. What really worried me, however, was the possibility of a tunnel looming up ahead. In such an event I intended to attempt a stalled turn, without losing enough height to hit the rails, and all being well, follow the railway back to Gaya.

So far there had been no trains and no overhead bridges either.

After twisting about for an interminable time, the curves became less acute and not so continuous. Heavily clad jungle country eventually replaced the hills, still the rain poured from above with the same monotonous intensity, enshrouding everything beyond a radius of 300 feet more or less.

I had seen heavy tropical rain in North Queensland, but nothing like this devastating deluge. The strain of keeping the railway in sight eased considerably when the line reached level country, indicated by the absence of cuttings.

Now that the railway was more or less straight, I eased the throttle forward to cruising speed and taking a quick glance at the clock, was surprised to see that over two and a half hours had slipped by since the rain had started and 5 hours 55 minutes had elapsed since leaving Jhansi. At least a quarter of an hour longer than it would have taken to reach Calcutta had the Swift maintained the speed at which it was travelling before meeting the rain.

So much time had probably been wasted following the railway at reduced speed, that Calcutta might still be anything from 80 to 100 miles away.

Soon after reaching the plains, I passed over a train going my way and for a few seconds the line was obscured by smoke and steam. Then to my dismay, a mile or so further on, a light mist appeared, rising from the ground to a height of about 20 feet, where it seemed to be held down by the rain. The railway could still be seen directly below, but it had been blotted out ahead. Back came the throttle again until the Swift was cruising at 70 miles per hour, at which speed it was possible to keep in sight the telegraph lines, (at the side of the railway) which projected above the mist.

The tops of two, sometimes three telegraph poles could be seen ahead as, mile after mile, they unwound in front, slipping by only a few feet below the Swift and still the rain came down.

This sort of flying was beginning to wear me down, it was becoming difficult to concentrate, difficult to fight against the desire to take my eyes away from those seemingly endless telegraph poles and the wires joining them.

Suddenly there were no more poles, I glanced down, the railway had disappeared, there was only an opaque void below, even the shadowy shape of the jungle on either side of the aircraft had vanished leaving nought but the horizontal daggers of rain spearing this purgatory.

Before I had time to figure out what could have happened, trees appeared ahead so abruptly I instinctively rammed the throttle wide and pulled the Swift into a steep climb. The Swift shot like a rocket into dense overcast.

For a split second I was terror-stricken. Then the idea occurred, that I must attempt to find the railway which had disappeared so suddenly.

The next lucid recollection was of the Swift breaking through the overcast, over a stretch of water and a few yards from the shore. The mist was no longer a menace, but rain still poured from above, severely limiting visibility.

With no clear plan, I followed the shore. Quickly glancing at the compass I was surprised to see the aircraft was on a southerly heading. On my right, water stretched away until hidden by the rain, on my left were buildings. Then a bridge loomed out of the murk ahead. The Hooghli bridge. By the grace of God I had reached Calcutta, but the way to Dum Dum aerodrome on the other side of the city was barred by cloud and rain.

After an attempt to cross the city and nearly colliding with the slender extrusion of a religious edifice pointing the way to heaven, I returned to the bridge, rather shaken by my narrow escape.

Despite the heavy rain, an ever increasing crowd gathered on the bridge as I circled a few feet above, debating whether to continue circling until the weather improved or more likely the Swift ran out of fuel, or attempt to reach Dum Dum by climbing high enough to clear any obstructions enroute.

The latter course meant entering the cloud and should my reckoning be faulty, the possibility of wrecking the Swift when descending.

Staying above the bridge was just as hazardous. When the Swift ran out of fuel, forcing me to 'ditch' in the muddy waters of the Hooghli about two hours hence.

The thought of being stranded in Calcutta, caused me to make another attempt to reach Dum Dum beneath the cloud base. A few minutes later I was back circling the bridge, prepared for the worst.

A crowd again gathered below, reminding me of a flock of crows hanging around an injured sheep. The thought that I was the one who was to provide the feast for their morbid curiosity rather annoyed me.

The continuous circling at such a low level was beginning to affect me and my handling of the aircraft became so faulty that I began to doubt my ability to continue until the fuel ran out.

In desperation, I decided to have another shot at reaching Dum Dum. This time at a safe height over the built up area of the city. Although the aerodrome was only a few miles away and I knew the direction, the possibility of finding the place under these atrocious conditions was far from bright, but it seemed to me the lesser of two evils.

Opening up the throttle, I climbed the Swift to a 1,000 feet heading on, what I hoped was, the correct course, cruised at that level for three minutes, then throttling back and gliding the aircraft at 60 miles per hour down to 400 feet, where I opened the throttle slightly and eased the stick back to slow the descent, transferring my gaze from the altimeter, when it showed 300 feet, to look out ahead.

Half blinded by the rain and sweating at the palms, I watched and waited. Ages seemed to pass before the Swift was through the cloud and descending rapidly on to the top of rain drenched trees.

No more than five feet separated the Swift from the vegetation by the time its glide had been broken and it was cruising level.

As far as it could be seen, vegetation stretched in every direction. My navigation had not been accurate enough to locate the aerodrome which could be anywhere within a radius of two miles or even more, and in any direction.

The clearance between the cloud base and the trees was too small to manoeuvre the Swift except in very gentle turns, making it well nigh impossible to make a thorough search.

Whilst I was deciding what to do, a clearing appeared stretching ahead until obscured by rain. Pulling the throttle back, instantly, I put the Swift into a steep sideslip. In my anxiety to get the aircraft down as quickly as possible I flattened out too abruptly causing the Swift to stall several feet above the earth. Quickly, I pushed the throttle forward and although the engine responded immediately, the Swift continued to sink towards the surface, which I discovered, to my horror, to be a lake.

Realising, with the engine flat out, the Swift would nose over when the wheels met the water, I cut the switches.

A fraction of a second later the wheels hit and a sheet of water came up and over the aircraft, half drowning me. The nose started to go down, then the tail dropped.

A miracle had happened. The Swift was still right side up, above water and apparently in one piece.

Shaking like a jolted jelly, I sat gazing at the deluge drumming on the wings and splashing into the water below. The lake in which the Swift had alighted extended in every direction as far as the rain would allow me to see, except behind the Swift where about 100 yards away, trees showed dimly through the rain.

Getting out of the Swift into water about 9 inches deep, I changed my saturated carpet slippers for shoes, fitted the engine and cockpit covers, then set off to look for help, making for the trees.

Loth to venture into the trees, I skirted alongside them, where the ground though saturated, was particularly clear of water.

After a few minutes walk, a building showed up. A hangar with its doors wide open revealing several aircraft. The lake in which I had alighted was the inundated surface of Dum Dum aerodrome.

As soon as I recognised where I was, I started to return to the aircraft. Although it was no more than 600 yards away, the walk seemed endless and the effort to remove the covers and restart the engine, exhausting.

Although the water covering the surface varied in depth, it was not too difficult to taxi the aircraft to the hangar. Here I managed to switch off the engine, but 'for the life of me', I was unable to get out of the cockpit. The battery, clutch or whatever it is that activates the nerves and muscles functioned no longer.

Still capable of thought, my mind, strangely enough, was unable to control my body.

The rain poured down, cascading off my helmet on to my knees, whilst I sat like a 'Zombi'.

After a while one of the aerodrome staff seeing the Swift standing on the tarmac ran over and shouted 'How did you get here?'

Incapable of speech, I gazed at the fellow, who after peering at me closely, asked if I was alright and where had I come from, shaking my shoulder as he did so.

The shake must have rattled my brain into gear again because I answered both his questions.

Getting out of the cockpit, I took off my helmet only to be advised to replace it again, because of the likelihood of getting sunstroke, despite the lack of sunshine.

Although drenched to the skin, I had no feeling of being wet, nor of being tired or hungry, in fact, I seemed bereft of sensibility, only vaguely aware that we had reached shelter, that I had changed my sodden clothing for a pair of khaki shorts and shirt.

It was not until I had eaten and swallowed several cups of coffee that I recovered enough to realise that my host was Mr Raynham, a well known pilot who was making a name for himself in the aviation world, with his air survey work in India.

He told me the atrocious weather was being caused by the south west monsoon, which as a rule ceased during October. That it might continue for days, again it might clear within a few hours. There was no means of knowing because meteorological information was sparse and often unreliable.

'I don't think the bad weather will extend beyond the coast', he continued. 'But the Sunderbans, between there and the Bay of Bengal are covered with impenetrable jungle, infested with tigers, where you wouldn't stand a chance of surviving if you should be forced down.'

'I strongly advise you to wait until the weather lifts so that you can fly over this area at a respectable height'. Raynham concluded.

Although this was interesting, my main concern was the condition of the aerodrome and I asked how long it would be, after the rain ceased, before it would be possible to take off.

Raynham said the ground was quite firm and the water drained away rapidly. 'In fact', he continued, 'there is a bit of a ridge in the middle of the 'drome which might be free enough of water to take off now'.

The ridge, which Raynham took me over to inspect, differed little in appearance from the remainder of the aerodrome. For approximately 100 yards, the ridge, if such it could be called, was practically free from water, except for a few puddles, then came a slight depression 2 or 3 inches deep in water, after that the ground was a few inches higher for another 30 yards or so before sloping to the inundated part of the ground. Not very good, but good enough to get the Swift off.

We were well and truly wet by the time we returned to the hangar, but my clothes had not been dried, so I changed as quickly as possible, anxious to get away from this enervating place, so hot and humid it was difficult to breathe.

While I was changing, news came through that the K.L.M. Fokker which had stayed the night at Allahabad, on its way to Batavia had been unable to get through the storm and had returned to Allahabad. Its skipper having more sense than I.

After taxying the Swift across the lake that was Dum Dum aerodrome, I eventually found the ridge. It might well have been out in the middle of the Indian Ocean for all that could be seen.

The period from the start of a takeoff until a height of 400 or 500 feet is reached, is perhaps the most critical part of any flight.

Many pilots, including myself, aware of the potential hazards during this period, are inclined to be tense immediately prior to takeoff. A similar feeling to that when one is about to plunge into cold water.

Although this particular takeoff promised to be most unpleasant, the usual pre-flight tension was absent when I pushed the throttle open. The Swift responded sluggishly, gathering speed too slowly to become airborne before reaching the depression, where the water retarded the aircraft almost tipping it on to its nose.

Clearing the depression, the Swift again gathered speed, almost attaining flying speed by the time it reached the end of the ridge. The wheels hit the water with a mighty splash. I pulled the stick back as I felt the nose 'peck'.

The Swift leaped into the air, returning to earth, with a mighty splash and thump, after flying a few yards.

Bounding into the air again, the Swift continued on its way, hopping like a kangaroo, then after aquaplaning for a few yards, finally staggered into the air in a semi-stalled condition.

Flying at last, but only just, the Swift faced another hazard, the palm fringed boundary that appeared out of the murk ahead.

The only sensible thing to have done in the circumstances was to have landed immediately, instead I allowed the Swift to continue sluggishly on its way, whilst calmly observing the approach to what appeared certain disaster.

Seemingly in slow motion the distance closed until the Swift was within a few yards of the trees, still below their tops.

Then when a collision looked inevitable, the Pobjoy seemed to exert a little extra power, lifting the Swift clear of the palms by the narrowest of margins.

Fully aware of my narrow escape, I eased the Swift out of its climb, with its wings scraping the cloud base, turned on course for Rangoon, automatically throttling the engine back to cruising speed.

Palms soon gave way to thick jungle which merged with the rain less than a mile ahead. The trees were fairly uniform in height, so that it was not difficult to keep the Swift under the cloud base, between 30 to 40 feet above the top of the jungle.

Occasionally I took a fleeting glance at the compass, to find its needle steady and parallel to the grid. The other instruments were also motionless, their indicators seemingly frozen in their correct positions. Even the Swift gave the impression that it had become immobile, halted by the stabbing darts of rain shooting through the sultry air, keeping pace with the jungle slipping by a few feet below.

For an indeterminable time, I sat motionless, devoid of feeling. My mind, still with, but not of my body, seemed to have shed its responsibilities of effective activation. A static condition which caused me not the slightest concern.

Mile after mile the monotonous scene unfolded with nothing to disturb my tranquility. This trance-like state was suddenly shattered when the Swift shot abruptly out of the murk into clear sky.

Less than 150 feet below the waters of the Bay of Bengal lapped the edge of the Sunderbans. Immediately behind, the cloud, like a mighty slate cliff, towered to tremendous heights, casting its shadow many miles over the sea ahead. Released from limbo, my mind commenced functioning normally again.

First thought was to put a bit of space between the Swift and the sea. At 6,000 feet the cool air soon made me aware of my sodden state. Before long I was half frozen and rather than face the risk of pneumonia, I took the Swift down to a lower altitude.

After two miserable hours, the Arakan coast showed away over to my left. Then I was stricken with a dreadful feeling of fatigue. With difficulty, I managed to get the Swift to Akyab, and vaguely remembered making a very bad landing and getting out of the aircraft. Then an instant later, or so it seemed, a young man whom I had not seen previously, was shouting and shaking me. He had been awakened, he said, by the keeper of the local rest house in which I was spending the night, who being unable to arouse me by shouting and banging on a gong - his religious scruples prevented him from touching me - had awakened the young man, who was in charge of the cable station about half a mile away, telling him, he feared I was ill or dead.

I had fallen asleep soon after arrival the previous day and had slept for ten hours.

Taking off from Akyab at 4.15am the Swift climbed through the cool, clear and calm pre-dawn atmosphere, so different from the heavy humid conditions experienced when leaving Jhansi, the previous morning.

The events of yesterday occupied my mind as the Swift climbed high over Combermere Bay, heading across the multitude of islands which lie off this part of the Burma coast.

My mental lapse just after arriving at Calcutta might well have been caused by fatigue from being without sleep since leaving Baghdad more than 54 hours previously. It was my subsequent frame of mind which puzzled me.

The change in mentality during my short stay in Calcutta, which had deprived me of all feeling, yet leaving me fully aware of all that was happening, also with the ability of still being able to handle the Swift.

My nonchalance during the hazardous takeoff at Dum Dum and indifference to the abominable conditions over the Sunderbans, surely had not been caused by fatigue.

My thinking about this matter was interrupted by the first flush of dawn, silhouetting the peaks of the Arakan Juma range which the Swift was approaching.

A few minutes later the sun came up 'like thunder above the road to Mandalay,' lighting up a bank of cloud towering in the west, at least a 100 miles away.

It was a joy to be aloft on such a glorious day, flying over this wild and beautiful region. A joy accentuated by thoughts of the breakfast I intended to eat when I reached Rangoon.

The rice paddies of the Irrawaddy Delta then came in sight to dominate the scene. Green fields stretching away to infinity, an incredible contrast to the scene of yesterday.

Although it was not yet 8 o'clock, the heat made itself felt as the Swift lost height on the descent to Rangoon. This colourful place glistening in the early morning sunlight brought to mind Athens, probably because of the vivid contrast between the two cities.

Ancient Athens with its dignified beauty enshrined by a stark mountainous landscape. Rangoon comparatively new and apparently ostentatious, surrounded by lush green plains, might well belong to a different world and another age.

These cities had one thing in common though! The most prominent edifice in Athens and the dominating Shive Dagan Pagoda in Rangoon had both been erected to glorify religion.

My approach to the landing ground was excellent. As the wheels skimmed the grass I congratulated myself on making a perfect landing. Then the Swift seemed to be sinking down through the earth. The view ahead disappeared and a fraction of a second later the Swift ceased its descent with a spine crinkling bump, then tore through grass at least six feet high, emerging eventually to an area of beautifully kept lawn, in the middle of which it came to rest, its undercarriage and wing struts festooned with grass, a considerable amount of which was wound around the propeller.

Whilst I was removing the grass, an elderly man approached and ordered me to take my 'contraption' away immediately.

Astonished and annoyed by this unreasonable demand, I replied that I would as soon as the Swift had been refuelled.

'There is no fuel here, so be off with you', the irate fellow said.

Before leaving London, I had been assured that fuel would be available at every potential port of call, including Rangoon. To be stranded for want of fuel and oil after getting this far, was a frustrating state of affairs.

I explained this to the unfriendly person now facing me in such a bellicose manner. He asked if I had really come from London.

When I told him I had departed from England the previous Saturday, the old man thawed considerably. He became quite nostalgic and started to tell me the story of his youth, spent within the sound of the Bow Bells.

With difficulty I managed to interrupt his reminiscence, making another plea for fuel and something to eat.

The old 'Cockney' then explained that I was on the polo ground, where I had no right to be, because a new aerodrome had just been built on the northern outskirts of the city, where I would probably get what I wanted.

Saying 'farewell' to the old fellow who now seemed reluctant for me to go, I wasted no time in taking off in search of the aerodrome, puzzled that it was not marked on the map, which distinctly showed the landing place to be the ground from which I had just departed.

The authorities at the new aerodrome had guessed what had happened when they had seen me fly over on my way in to Rangoon, and when I failed to reappear within a reasonable time, had wondered if I had come to grief on the erstwhile landing ground.

My explanation, that the polo ground was marked on my map as the aerodrome, did not surprise them. They expected, in due course, the Government of Burma would get around to notifying the world at large, that Rangoon now possessed a new and up-to-date airport, 'so that the Rangoon Polo Club would no longer suffer the invasion of their domain by ignorant aeronauts'.

After a marvellous breakfast, I was presented (despite my protest that I was a strict total abstainer) with a small flask of brandy, by a charming lady, who stated 'All aviators should carry such a stimulant in the event of becoming faint when flying a long distance'.

Despite the delay caused by my landing on the polo ground, the Swift was in the air again by 9.25am (local time) and within a few minutes had crossed the Burma coast, heading out over the Gulf of Mataban for King Island where I expected to make a landfall within three hours. Apart from the Timor Sea, the 310 miles of ocean ahead, was the longest stretch of open water between here and Australia, therefore I had taken great care checking my course and orienting the aircraft on the run from Rangoon to the coast. I could, of course, have cut across the top of the bay to Moulmein, then down the coast, but this would have placed Singora - which I hoped to reach that night - beyond the range of the Swift.

Going out to sea no longer affected me as it had done when I set out to cross the Ligurian Sea. Although on crossings with the weather fine and calm, there was nothing to do except keeping the compass needle aligned with its grid and occasionally pumping a few gallons of fuel from the auxiliary to the main tank, there was always plenty to think about.

Today, poised apparently motionless between sea and sky, I wondered how fast the Swift was really moving through space. This mental exercise kept me busy for about two hours, during which time the Swift had probably travelled 220,000 or more miles towards eternity and 200 miles towards its destination.

By this time the Moscos Archipelago should have been in sight about 20 miles away to the east. These were obscured by a haze which had reduced visibility to about 15 miles, otherwise flying conditions were perfect.

Failure to sight these islands caused me no concern, but an hour later, when by my reckoning I should have been over King Island, the sight of nothing except sea and sky caused me some misgiving.

Aware that there had been a gradual deviation of the compass since leaving England, I had oriented the Swift after every takeoff, except that from Calcutta and so far this method had been quite satisfactory.

Another ten minutes ticked by without a sight of land to curb my mounting anxiety. With the Swift maintaining its correct heading, the present position could have been caused by a change in the wind.

The Rangoon forecast had been for light and variable winds tending S.S.E. Either the wind had moved to the east blowing the Swift further out to sea or had turned into a strong headwind.

In either case, the possibility of reaching Singora before running out of fuel, seemed very remote. The most important factor however, was to determine my position, as soon as possible, by changing direction towards the mainland, somewhere to the east.

As I brought the Swift round on to the new course, a small island appeared ahead and a few seconds later, hills appeared about ten miles away to the right.

Changing back on to the original course, I soon discovered the hills were on King Island. The Swift had taken 40 minutes longer than estimated to make the sea crossing.

With no possibility of reaching Singora with the fuel remaining, I altered course for Victoria Point, taking the Swift down to 4,000 feet, hoping, at that level, to escape the worst of the headwind.

The Sun low in the west, was casting long shadows when the Swift eventually reached Victoria Point, which apart from the wireless station, showed little of itself.

A few miles north of the village, the landing ground, surrounded by hills looked so uninviting, that despite the risk of a night landing, I would have continued onto Singora had there been sufficient fuel to do so.

Touching down on the small narrow strip was easy against the steady southerly breeze, but I had grave misgivings about getting the Swift airborne again. The surface, although well grassed, was rough in parts, the main worry, however, was the approaches. The strip sloped uphill to the southern boundary, beyond this rising timber precluded a safe takeoff with full load, even against the wind. Taking off in the other direction downhill with a tailwind would be just as hazardous.

Unless the wind dropped or changed direction, it would be necessary to take the Swift off, as lightly laden as possible, with only sufficient fuel to reach Singora. This would mean delaying my proposed departure for 2 hours, to arrive at Singora at daybreak.

This delay and the extra time refuelling at Singora would make it impossible to reach Cheribon tomorrow. In fact, should the headwind, which had retarded the Swift today, still persist, I might not get beyond Singapore.

These miserable thoughts were dispelled by the arrival of the fuel merchant who, ignoring my request to fill only the main tank, filled both tanks to overflowing.

Very annoyed by this disregard of my instructions, I explained the reason for requiring the limited amount of fuel. An explanation brushed aside by the fuel man who, in quaint English, blandly assured me that the atmosphere would be absolutely dormant when the time came for me to depart, and that there would be no difficulty in taking the air by running the flying machine down hill.

Whether this assurance was due to the man's knowledge of the weather or his mercenary intent, will never be known.

After tying the Swift down, I was taken to a resthouse by a young English engineer from the radio station, which I learned was the most powerful in the India-Burma area.

I was invited to dine at the radio station at 8 o'clock that night and told not to worry about dressing. A remark which puzzled me at the time.

The dinner was excellent and most enjoyable, although, at first, I felt rather out of place in my grubby clothes amongst the formally dressed company which was predominantly Indian.

Discussion ranged on many matters of world interest. An unexpected pleasure was the discussion on aviation with the wide knowledge of this subject displayed by the Indian manager of the wireless station, an Oxford graduate who, I afterwards learned, was one of the most outstanding radio engineers in the Empire.

Time passed so quickly it was eleven o'clock before I returned to the rest-house, hoping to get a couple of hours rest. Unfortunately the humid heat prevented me from sleeping, consequently, I was ready and waiting when the Englishman called at 1am to take me out to the landing ground.

Despite the early hour, a number of natives came to see me off, one of them being unkind enough to souvenir my carpet slippers while I was checking over the engine.

Those slippers had been a godsend during the flight so far, and I was loth to go without them, but my appeal for them to be returned was in vain.

The prediction of the fuel merchant proved correct, not a breath of air disturbed the atmosphere.

The hills surrounding the landing ground presented a problem, being too high for sighting a star to keep the aircraft straight during takeoff.

There were no flares available, but a lantern was procured and taken down to the far end of the field by one of the local lads.

Taking off, with the heavy load, over the rough ground was rather alarming. Every second I expected the fire damaged strut to collapse. Then, shortly after the tail lifted, the aircraft appeared to swing to the right, but as I kicked on left rudder to align the nose with the light, the Swift became airborne, whilst the light continued to veer away to the left. Apparently the approaching roar of the Swift frightened the lantern holder, who suddenly abandoned his post as the aircraft raced towards him.

A few seconds later the climbing Swift narrowly missed the hillside, or so it seemed to me, as I banked the aircraft away from the hazard.

From Victoria Point it was a continuous climb to 10,000 feet to clear the Kiong-ga Tock range, the tops of which appeared to be enshrouded in cloud.

Several hours later dawn came with the Swift over a cloud covered Siam. Never before had I seen such fantastic formations in the sky. Towering mountains of slate grey cloud, changing gradually to a lighter hue with the coming of daylight, as yet not strong enough to penetrate the chasms of jet separating jagged vaporous peaks and frowning precipices, with white castles whose pinnacles were tinged with delicate rose. Most spectacular of all, a mighty vapour lion, with gaping jaws and misty mane faced east, seemingly waiting to seize the Sun just appearing above the horizon, to bathe the bizarre scene in crimson and gold. An enthralling sight which amply compensated me for the trials and tribulations so far suffered on this adventure.

Soon the scene bleached until the white masses were so dazzling to the eyes, I decided to descend through a gap in the clouds, finding below heavy jungle out of which reared grotesque limestone mountains, their vertical sides bare and white, contrasting strangely with the verdant growth covering their tops.

Then another unusual sight appeared in the shape of a giant three engined Fokker which passed within a quarter of a mile, heading north, perhaps for Bangkok, on the weekly service between Amsterdam and Batavia. The first aircraft I had seen in the air since leaving Britain.

A strange coincidence for two of the world's most modern vehicles to meet over this wild, isolated country devoid of any visible means of surface transport.

After nearly four hours in the air, a plume of smoke to the southwest indicated Penang the first sign of habitation so far that day. The smoke had barely faded from sight when I was forced to climb the Swift to 8,000 feet to clear the Bukit Panjong mountains. Awe inspiring country, but most unsuitable for forced landings.

Signs of civilization appeared about 40 minutes later when the Swift flew over the village of Ipoh, where it may have been possible to have landed on one or two clearings in the vicinity. A joy to the eye after flying for several hundred miles over 'tiger country'.

Soon after passing Kuala Lumpur, an attractive little town nestling in the hills, the air became turbulent and heavy rain battered the Swift.

That this time of the year was supposed to be the dry season in the India - Malay area, made me wonder what the wet season would be like. How K.L.M. managed to operate a regular scheduled service, the year round, in such atrocious weather, was beyond my comprehension.

The Dutch pilots must be a tough lot and the Fokker aircraft they flew, in a class of their own, to endure such conditions, month in month out.

The bad weather continued to within fifty miles of Singapore when the clouds suddenly vanished.

Although the Swift had covered this stage in good time, the whole journey, so far, had been much slower than anticipated. Had it been possible to adhere to the original schedule, the Swift would have been over 1,200 miles further on, nearing Bino instead of approaching Singapore, which had just appeared ahead.

Exactly 6 hours 50 minutes after leaving Victoria Point, the Swift touched down at Seletar aerodrome, the Royal Air Force base at Singapore.

This, my first contact with the Royal Air Force, will long be remembered by me. Refuelling was commenced as soon as the propeller stopped revolving. Seconds later engineers and riggers were making a complete check of the aircraft. Mentioning the suspect compass. I was told it would be swung and corrected if time permitted.

I was taken to the quarters for a bath and breakfast, then I paid my respects to the commanding officer, returning to the tarmac within 45 minutes. Less than 50 minutes after arrival the Swift was back in the air, clean as a new pin and heading for Java.

The sergeant who had been in charge of the work on the Swift hadn't the time to correct the compass in the period at his disposal, he was able, however, to put the Swift on the swinging base and check the compass on the 90° - 180° quadrant, afterwards compiled a new deviation card covering the points in this arc, which encompassed the two long sea crossings I had yet to make. The deviation which varied from between 16° and 20° was thought to have been caused by the loss of magnetism in the large petrol tank installed a few inches away from the compass.

The Swift took off from Seletar into a strong northerly breeze which was driving a heavy rain storm over the aerodrome boundary. The aerodrome was so large, however, sufficient height had been gained to turn the aircraft on course before reaching the rain. The way over Singapore was clear, and beyond, Bulang Island, directly on track, could be seen, enabling me to make an accurate check of the course and prove the accuracy of the new deviation card.

Fifty minutes out from Singapore the Swift flew over Lingga Island and the Equator, and Winter became Summer, not that any difference could be noticed. Climatically summer started on the door step to Arabia, so far as I was concerned. Except during the nights at Baghdad and Jask, the temperature since leaving Aleppo had varied from very warm to exceedingly hot. The Swift was slow to reach Banka Island and when it did, eventually, it was several miles to the west of its track. The wind had switched round to the southwest making the possibility of reaching Cheribon, that night, very remote.

During the 15 minutes it took to cross the island, the ground wind changed direction several times. By the time the south coast of the island was reached the wind had backed to the north east, pushing the Swift along over the 30 miles of open water to Sumatra in 16 minutes, raising my hopes of reaching Cheribon after all.

For the next hour the Swift flew over the most dismal stretch of country I have ever seen. A steamy hell of swampy mangroves, so repulsive, I shuddered at the thought of being forced down on such forbidding terrain, although no worse, probably, than the Sunderbans, which were mercifully hidden when I passed over.

Today the atmosphere was remarkably clear, although a bank of clouds was peeping over the horizon, many miles ahead, their jagged tops reminding me of the Warrumbungles.

The Java Sea showed up at last, the open water a welcome sight after traversing those sinister Sumatran swamps, even the cloud, a giant curtain stretching from horizon to horizon, barring the way about 20 miles ahead, did not daunt me, although it extended up to tremendous heights from a base so low and rain enshrouded it seemed to blend with the sea. Slate grey at low levels with snowy white peaks reaching well beyond the ultimate ceiling of the Swift.

Hoping to find a way over this barrier, I climbed the Swift until, fifteen minutes later the aircraft reached 12,000 feet and was within a mile of the towering mass. Turning the aircraft to port I flew parallel to the cloud, searching in vain for an opening for about ten minutes, then turning about, spent another 20 minutes exploring in the other direction.

Flashes of lightning frequently lit up the cloud alongside, and occasionally a flash would escape the cloud, penetrating the clear sky like the flick of a snakes tongue, as I took the Swift back towards sea level.

Down at 4,000 feet all signs of lightning ceased, giving the impression the intense electrical activity was confined to high levels.

Thinking it might be possible to get through under the worst of the storm, I decided to brave the elements rather than return over that dreadful swamp to seek a landing in Sumatra until the weather improved.

Almost immediately after turning back on course, the Swift was enveloped in dense cloud, where the air was so smooth, I began to think the appearance of the storm had been deceptive. Then a strange thing happened, the altimeter needle started moving round in an upward direction much faster than I had ever seen before. At first I thought the instrument had gone 'haywire'. The gradual falling off of the indicated airspeed and peculiar feeling in my head, soon proved otherwise.

The Swift was ascending at an incredible rate, yet so smoothly it was hard to believe any change was taking place. Without a tittle of turbulence, the altimeter needle passed the 8,000 feet mark, the aircraft having mounted 4,000 feet in no more than a minute.

Instinctively I throttled the engine back and eased the stick forward to maintain flying speed, but the altimeter continued to mount the scale, 9,000 feet, then 10,000 feet were soon passed.

An ascent of 6,000 feet in less than two minutes. The last 2,000 feet with the engine throttled back. This was too much to believe.

The altimeter must have gone wrong and the Swift instead of mounting heavenward, might well be heading for the ocean since the engine had been throttled, a thought which caused me to open up the engine to cruising speed. The altimeter now showed 11,000 feet. Here the cloud was almost as black as night. Occasionally a vivid flash would light up the Swift with such intensity, the following darkness seemed more intense.

Fear replaced amazement as the Swift continued to rise. I began to wonder if the legendary gods of old really existed and this was a demonstration of their power or had the Earth's gravity ceased to exist, allowing centrifugal force to hurl the Swift out into space enclosed in a vaporous mass which might once have been the sea below. Were other people and objects being cast off the planet, leaving some trapped on the ceilings of homes and offices until the 'crack of doom'.

These ludicrous thoughts were interrupted by the Swift dropping suddenly and so violently it seemed as if the safety harness would ram my shoulders on to my hips.

As the aircraft fell, a flash of lightning (followed instantly by a clap of thunder which made my head sing) lit the aircraft so brilliantly that for several seconds I was unable to see the instruments, not that I could do anything but sit like a hypnotised rabbit waiting for the end.

Seconds later the Swift halted its plunge with such a severe jolt, I thought at first the aircraft had hit the sea. Then the Swift was rocketing heavenward again. Although terrified, sufficient wit remained for me to open up the engine periodically to keep the temperature sufficiently high to prevent the engine from 'petering out'.

Keeping the speed of the aircraft within reasonable limits was well nigh impossible. Despite my efforts the air speed course of the Swift had also become erratic; it was beyond my ability to follow the wild oscillations of the compass and the needle of the turn and bank indicator, with the aircraft behaving like a demented dolphin.

The magnitude of movement both up and down, with the consequent rapidity of load reversal must surely break the little Swift before long. But there was nothing I could do about getting out of this situation, because with the compass behaving the way it was, it was impossible to tell any direction except up and down.

After enduring this purgatory for over an hour, the Swift still intact, suddenly shot out of the storm, seemingly none the worse for the battering it had received. I had not fared so well. My shoulders were raw from the chafing of the harness, the knuckles of my left hand had been 'barked', my head ached and my posterior was so sore I might well have been kicked through the storm, also I had the impression that my inside was quivering like a jelly.

At first I was unsure whether the Swift had emerged from the storm on the side it had entered or had gone through to the far side. The Sun was hidden by the bank of cloud which towered above, however when the compass needle settled down, it was about 15° out of alignment with the grid.

Relieved to discover Java was somewhere ahead and not on the other side of the cloud bank, I wasted no time in bringing the Swift back on to course.

Within a few minutes the Swift was far enough away from the clouds for the sun to appear. To my surprise its bearing from the aircraft had changed by at least 50° to that prior to entering the storm. In my addled state of mind, I considered whether the sun had, unaccountably, been misplaced in heaven (after my recent experience nothing would have surprised me) or did the compass err.

Fortunately, I had retained sufficient sense to realise that something must have happened to the compass. Deciding to ignore this fickle aid, I altered course until the sun's bearing was relative to that prior to encountering the storm. Continuing on a steady track by keeping constant the shadow on the windscreen.

This crude method of navigation was not very accurate because of the gradual movement of the sun, it would, however, enable me to make a landfall somewhere on the Java coast.

Very little turbulence disturbed the air, and although it was hazy, the weather was so good now, it was hard to realise such terrifying conditions prevailed only a few miles astern.

The existence of forces able to fling a machine weighing a thousand pounds or so, upwards for several thousand feet, as if it were no more than a piece of thistle-down, was so fantastic, it would be doubtful if anyone would have believed such a thing could happen.

Only for the evidence of bleeding knuckles and other painful reminders, I, myself, might well have attributed the memory of my recent experience to imagination, kindled by the capricious behaviour of the Swift's instruments.

Within 15 minutes the compass needle had moved approximately 20° back towards the true course. Ignoring this I continued to use the sun, now sinking to the west, as my guide, expecting to sight Java any time from now on.

Then the engine coughed, causing me to glance at the fuel gauge which should have shown the main tank to have been at least half full, instead it registered empty.

The engine coughed again and then 'petered out'. Quickly, I started pumping what remained in the auxiliary tank into the main, as the Swift glided down towards the sea 5,400 feet below. At 4,000 feet the engine 'picked up', coughed a couple of times, then ran smoothly.

The auxiliary tank soon ran out, but there was not sufficient fuel in the main tank to reach Batavia if the Swift was anywhere near its correct track. What concerned me was the possibility of the main tank having sprung a leak during the battering the Swift had received recently.

I had topped up the main tank immediately prior to entering the storm. During the intervening period it would have been impossible for the engine to have consumed such a large quantity.

There was no smell of fuel or any other indication of a petrol leak, but it was quite possible for the slipstream to whisk away fuel escaping in small quantities unseen and unsmelled.

Another 30 minutes went by without a sign of land, my anxiety mounting with the passing of each minute. By now the Swift had been in the air for nearly six and a half hours and should have reached the coast at least half an hour previously.

Ten minutes later when the lower limb of the sun was about to dip into the sea, the Swift flew over a small island, on which a lighthouse stood, then another island appeared through the haze followed by several others. The Thousand Islands.

A few minutes later the Java coast showed up, then the lights of Batavia appeared ahead and soon after I sighted the aerodrome.

The Swift touched down as the last of daylight vanished, having taken 7 hours 5 minutes to cover the 580 miles from Singapore.

After being greeted by several charming Dutchmen (I never learned how they knew I would be calling at Batavia seeing that Cheribon was my objective when I left Singapore) I made a thorough examination of the Swift, which appeared to have suffered little damage from the storm. The aileron wires were slacker than normal. There was no sign of a fuel leak although there were no more than two gallons remaining on arrival. The only explanation I could think of for the disappearance of at least 8 gallons of fuel was that it had been sucked out through the vent pipe on the top of the main tank during the violent down draughts experienced in the storm.

The Swift had proved itself to be an outstanding aircraft, not only for withstanding the battering it had received, but also for its stability under the most shocking conditions. An aircraft which could be flown with confidence anywhere, in any weather, but never again by me. I intended to keep well clear of thunderstorms in the future.

Not being able to reach Cheribon that night was unfortunate, because the range of the Swift was too short to fly non-stop to Bima from here. Faced with an additional stop for fuel, I decided to refuel at Sourabaya instead of Cheribon. This would enable me to make an earlier start, which would be necessary if Koepang was to be reached by the following night.

I was taken to a magnificent marble palace - or so it seemed to me - in Batavia, where after a hot bath, I slipped into my pyjamas and then bed to 'repair nature with comforting repose'.

My Dutch host had other ideas. Despite my pleas for sleep, he insisted that I appear at a dinner party he was giving in my honour. That I had not slept since leaving Akyab over 36 hours ago, had flown for 14 hours that day, in addition to being half frightened to death, meant nothing to him. He was only concerned about his party at which he hoped I would entertain his guest with tales of adventure.

'A drop of Schiedam is all you want to put you right', he said.

Lacking the endurance or maybe the moral courage to prolong the argument, I allowed myself to be garbed in a flamboyant dressing gown and a pair of slippers too large for me and with great reluctance was led by my host to the festive table where I felt quite out of place, seated between two bejewelled women whose attempts to converse in a quaint mixture of Dutch and English embarrassed me considerably, not knowing whether they were speaking to me or conversing with each other.

The whole affair seemed as incongruous as a Lewis Carrol tea party. I remembered vaguely my host making a speech during which I must have gone to sleep, because my next recollection was of being in a comfortable bed, being shaken by someone who was shouting 'Awaken! Awaken'.

The previous evening I had mentioned I would have to take off at two o'clock the following morning to reach Koepang the same day.

Within a few minutes I had dressed and had been conducted back to the party, still going at full throttle in spite of it being a few minutes after 1 a.m.

As soon as I appeared, those who were capable wished me 'bon voyage', and after drinking a cup of excellent coffee, I was escorted to an ancient vehicle, my host explaining it would be safer for me to be conveyed to the aerodrome by taxi, rather than suffer the risk of being driven there by himself or his friends, whose ability and mobility had been somewhat impaired by the night's celebrations.

They intended, however to see me take off. A merry party piled into the decrepit taxi, despite the mumbled protests of its driver.

Barely a mile had been covered before a tyre blew out with a loud bang, which set all the dogs in the neighbourhood, barking.

The driver got out of the car in a leisurely manner and surveyed the damaged tyre, scratching his head and other parts of his anatomy, whilst my host and his friends verbally blasted him in Dutch, or maybe Malay. I looked on wondering why nothing was being done about changing the tyre.

At last, when the invective ceased, I was told there was no spare tyre nor any tools to change it if there had been.

Had I known the way and had been less tired, I could have walked to the aerodrome in less time than it took the taxi to make the journey on a flat tyre.

This annoying incident ruled out any possibility of reaching Koepang before nightfall or of arriving at Darwin at daybreak the next day.

After checking the fuel tanks to satisfy myself there had been no leakage during the night, I eventually got away at 4.30am, two and a half hours later than I had planned.

The flight to Sourabaya was uneventful, although heavy storms accompanied by vivid displays of lightning, were active over the mountains a few miles south of my track.

The sun rose about an hour after leaving Batavia, lighting up the lush country below. A few minutes later the Swift crossed the coast a little to the north of Cheribon.

Over the following 140 miles the route lay parallel to and a few miles north of the shore, which, with its backdrop of cloud crowned mountains, presented a scene of rare beauty.

Although the sun was shining when the Swift left Sourabaya, when the Swift touched down on the aerodrome, on the western outskirts, large banks of ominous looking clouds were building up, far beyond, in the southeast, causing a feeling of apprehension about future progress.

Yesterday's experience had dampened all desire for flying in clouds. So far as I was concerned, in the future I would be emulating the birds, who wisely refrained from flying when they were unable to see.

Only my intense desire to reach Tooraweenah as soon as possible prevented me from staying at Sourabaya (an attractive looking place), until the way ahead was free of cloud.

Half an hour after my arrival, the Swift had been fuelled and the engine started, when the caretaker of the aerodrome demanded a fee, the equivalent of 4 pounds before he would allow me to depart.

With less than 4 pounds in my pocket, this demand caused me acute embarrassment. Departing from England with ample funds - so I thought - to meet my needs en route, but the luxurious apartment, at the grand Hotel at Naples, had been very expensive and payments to the rest-house keepers at Akyab and Victoria Point had whittled the remainder to the paltry sum I now possessed.

My plea, that I was unable to pay the landing fee, fell on unsympathetic ears. The caretaker, quite irate, said I must pay the money before leaving.

Approaching the man who had refuelled the Swift, I appealed to him for help, but he seemed unable to understand my predicament.

Turning to the caretaker whose knowledge of English was better, I asked him to telephone the Vacuum Oil Company representative, who would undoubtedly guarantee payment of the fee. He told me the oil company did not open its office on Sundays and I would have to wait until the following day to get any money from them.

My assurance that the fee would be forwarded immediately after my arrival in Australia, met with a hostile response. I was curtly ordered to stop my engine. Instead, I jumped into the cockpit and took the Swift off without pausing to put on my flying cap or fasten the safety harness, doing so as soon as the Swift had gained sufficient height for me to take my hands from the controls.

This incident upset me so much, that Sourabaya looked far less attractive than hitherto. Apart from being an unpleasant episode, the trouble over the landing fee had caused an additional delay of 25 minutes. Sufficient time to allow the weather ahead to close in.

The likelihood of being held up at Bima, the next fuelling stop or at Koepang because of this incident, added to my discomfort.

An isolated storm was spilling a deluge of rain on Cape Tjina and the end of the Madura Strait beyond, forcing me to the south and over the strait of Bali. Over the Strait I took the Swift down to within 200 feet of the water, hoping to spot a tiger or two swimming the Strait, which the tigers did frequently according to my host in Batavia. Seeing no evidence of the animals, I came to the conclusion, 'my leg had been pulled'.

Except for a narrow strip of its southern coast, the Island of Bali was enshrouded in heavy cloud which soon extended out to sea, forcing me further south off the direct track to Bima.

I caught fleeting glimpses of the adjoining island Lombok, but was again forced south to avoid ominous storm clouds extending far out to sea.

This deterioration in the weather caused me some concern about locating Bima, which is situated at the head of a narrow bay on the north coast of Sumbawa Island.

Fortunately, by the time Allas Strait, the 20 miles strip of water separating Lombok from Sumbawa, was reached the cloud had lifted to about 3,000 feet on the coast although it was down on the ground a mile or so inland.

Eventually, the Swift reached Tiempia Bay, a landlocked sheet of water running inland in a northerly direction for about 15 miles. From the head of this bay Bima was less than 40 miles away. If a gap in the cloud could be found, it would be possible to reach Bima in a little over half an hour, whereas to continue around the coast through Sapir Strait to the northern side of the island would take at least an hour, perhaps longer should any storms block the way.

Deciding to attempt a crossing of the island, I flew along the eastern shore of the bay to its head. Here the cloud was down on the hills, but I found a gap through which I was able to squeeze the Swift with no more than 50 feet to spare.

Following a valley down to Bima, the Swift was over the village 5 hours after leaving Sourabaya and skimming the salt pan which served as a landing ground a few minutes later.

Immediately it stopped rolling the Swift was surrounded by dozens of dusky local citizens who seemed to have sprung out of the ground, to crowd around the aircraft until moved back by two Chinese who turned up to refuel the Swift a few minutes after my arrival.

Until reaching Batavia the Swift had remained remarkably clean. Here the oil tank had been overfilled, consequently a considerable amount of oil had been spilled over the engine cowlings. A mess I decided to clean up while the Swift was being refuelled.

As soon as I commenced cleaning the aircraft, the two Chinese abandoned the refuelling, one of them taking the cleaning rag from me firmly but politely. When I protested the elder Chinese explained, by eloquent signs, that I had committed a misdemeanour by soiling my hands.

Without one word being spoken, I was informed in no uncertain manner, that my activities on the ground must be confined to behaving like an aviator was expected to behave. In blunt English he meant. 'You stick to your job and let us do ours'.

After this superb exhibition of miming, the actor and his mate completed the refuelling and then did such a good job cleaning the Swift, it looked as good as new, except where it had been denuded of paint.

The work had been completed so quickly I was tempted to go on to Reo, a small town on the next island, Flores. With at least two hours of daylight remaining, it would have been easy to have flown the 125 miles before nightfall.

As I was about to start the engine, the spectators suddenly prostrated themselves facing a magnificent motor car which drew up a few yards from the Swift.

Out of the car emerged a person of imposing appearance, adorned in most ornate garb, who approached me through a lane of prostrate citizens, followed by two attendants.

This astounding spectacle of an eastern Potentate, surrounded by his obeisant vassals, seemed to belong to another age.

I might well have been a character of H.G. Wells creation and the Swift a time machine, which had taken me back to the ancient past, except for the motor car which seemed quite out of place in this bizarre scene.

In silence broken only by the call of a bird and the rustling of the breeze in the palms on the edge of the landing ground, the procession slowly advanced to within ten feet. Here the leader halted and bowed to me. Not to be outdone by such courtesy, I also bowed, a manoeuvre which reminded me that I had not eaten anything so far that day.

After this salutation had been indulged in several times, one of the attendants stepped forward, bowed and announced in a loud voice and the manner of a toast master at a Lord mayor's banquet. 'The Sultan of Bima presents his compliments per medium of his Prime Minister who has come in person to welcome you to the Sultan's domains. He wishes you well and commands that you be happy'.

This address, delivered in perfect English by a coffee coloured Oriental, rather surprised me. I tried to think of some flowery response to the speech, but words failed me. Instead I merely bowed to the Prime Minister. Several more bows were exchanged, then the attendant again addressed me. 'The Prime Minister desires that you accompany him in his automobile to Bima'.

Once more bows were exchanged. Then the Prime Minister turned about and the procession returned to the car, with me as rearguard, the idea of proceeding to Reo abandoned.

The Prime Minister was ceremoniously ushered into the rear seat of his car, a 1930 Buick. The aristocracy of this island certainly did themselves well, although I couldn't help thinking it would have been more appropriate had the Chief of State been ensconced in a howdah on the top of a white elephant.

The interpreter invited me to be seated alongside his 'Baas'. Before getting into the car, I asked about the safety of the Swift being left unattended at the mercy of such a large crowd.

'None will touch, they only look', was the reply.

The interpreter, who acted as driver and the other attendant occupied the front seat and the car moved off in low gear gradually attaining the speed of ten miles an hour.

Immediately he started, the driver became quite garrulous. He was a man of many parts, he informed me, holding other important positions besides those of interpreter and chauffeur. One of these being dancing master of the Sultanate.

He was a Malay, who had been brought from Singapore to teach dancing to the Ladies of the Sultan's harem. 'Jazz and all the latest steps you know', he enthusiastically explained.

The young Malay went on to describe other facets of his life, whilst the car rolled along through the jungle at little more than walking pace. He also spoke of future prospects including his desire and intention of marrying the daughter of the Prime Minister.

I cast a glance at the August gentleman beside me, to see his reaction to this piece of information, forgetting he knew no English. The elderly gentleman was apparently dozing.

After the car had ambled along for a considerable distance in low gear, I interrupted the voluble Malay to ask if he had forgotten to change gear.

'No I haven't', was the reply. 'The Prime Minister will not permit the automobile to proceed at more than ten miles per hour when he rides in it. But don't worry I will take you back to the aeroplane really fast tomorrow'.

Nearly half an hour passed, during which the Prime Minister sat motionless beside me and the driver chatted away in very good English, completely ignoring the fourth occupant of the car. Whether the Malay was trying to impress him with his command of English or merely practicing the language, was a matter for conjecture. Much of his conversation did not make sense to me and I was glad when I was finally deposited at the rest house, although rather disappointed by not being invited to meet the Sultan and his harem about whom I had heard so much of during the journey into Bima.

At the rest house there were more salutations and a promise from the Malay that he would call for me at 1.30 o'clock tomorrow morning and take me out 'really fast to the aeroplane'.

I reckoned on taking off at 2.30 a.m., to arrive over Ambogaga, on the south coast of Flores, just after dawn, so that I could obtain an accurate orientation before crossing the sea to Timor Island.

Without sustenance since gulping the cup of coffee at Batavia over 14 hours ago, the idea of drinking a large glass of milk, preferably chilled appealed to me immensely, so I lost no time in finding the dining room and approaching its sole occupant who was leaning on a broom, apparently daydreaming.

My request for a glass of milk was met by a stare. It was obvious the fellow knew no English. This reminded me of a slip of paper which had been given to me by my host in Batavia, who had become concerned when learned that I knew nothing of the Malay language.

He told me there were many places in the East Indian Archipelago, particularly east of Java where only Malay and local dialects were spoken and should I land in any of these places I would probably have difficulty in making myself understood.

Producing the paper on which the vocabulary had been written, I searched in vain for the word milk. Food, water, oil, petrol, night, bed, time and several other words were there with the Malayan translation alongside, but not milk. So I decided to settle for anything that would fill the void in the vicinity of my solar plexus.

The local lad eyed me warily as I read to him. 'Kassi makin'. 'Bring food'. Without a word he made a rapid exit thus raising my hopes of getting something to eat.

A few minutes later the broom boy returned with someone who addressed me in what may have been Dutch. I responded by asking in English for a glass of milk. With a look of bewilderment the newcomer shook his head. I then showed him my vocabulary pointing to the Malayan translation for food.

The fellow gazed at the point of my finger for a while, then took the paper, examined it on both sides and handed it back to me without so much as a word.

Thoroughly frustrated I wandered round the room silently cursing the Tower of Babel.

A number of glasses on the sideboard gave me the idea of emulating the Chinese at the aerodrome by attempting to obtain what I wanted by miming.

Picking up one of the glasses, I pretended to drink and then said. 'Milk please'. This brought some action, the older man said something to the broom boy who promptly disappeared, returning a few minutes later with a bottle of beer.

I shook my head and said 'No, I want milk please'.

A bottle of Schnapps and some water was produced.

It was a great temptation to take a drink of water, but I had been told that dire consequences could result from drinking unboiled water in this part of the world.

Denial of my thirst in this respect spurred me to fresh endeavour. Going over to a chair and seating myself, I beckoned to the elderly gent, who, with a look of surprise, came over and stood in front of me.

'Look!', I said slowly. 'I want some milk, which comes from a cow, an animal shaped like this'. I outlined, in the air, the shape of a cow, particularly its udder and teats. Then I gave a demonstration of milking the imaginary cow, even trying to imitate the peculiar sound of the milk striking the side of the bucket. I thought this was quite a realistic per- formance, it certainly held the attention of the man, who watched me intently, yet he showed no sign of understanding and when I ended my act by mooing in rather plaintive manner, the fellow jumped back a few feet, eyeing me suspiciously.

The noise I had made, brought a number of local lads hurrying into the room, where they formed a curious group.

Ignoring the look of consternation on the fellow in front of me, I repeated my performance, hoping that at least one of the newcomers had the intelligence and imagination to understand.

The gathering closed in. Those at the back pushing to get a better view as I gripped an imaginary bucket between my knees and pulled the imaginary teats.

All seemed intensely interested in the ridiculous pantomime, but none was amused. By their serious attitude, it was quite possible most, if not all, of them considered me insane. To be thus afflicted is of grave consequence and I had visions of being put under restraint, but despite this possibility I was determined to go through the act to the bitter end.

What seemed a lengthy silence followed my last 'Moo'. Then someone, either brighter or more knowledgeable then the rest of his companions, muttered. 'Soo soo' or something similar. A cry taken up by the rest of the gathering, which for some reason or the other became rather excited.

The look on the old fellow's face relaxed as he repeated the word and issued an order to the house boy.

Delicious thoughts of sipping a large glass of cool, creamy milk, allowing it to linger on my tongue, then slide gently down my throat to appease both my thirst and hunger, gave me a wonderful feeling of satisfaction, the result of my persistence. Which reminded me of a notation given to me many years ago by Frank Roberts:- "Nothing in the world can take the place of persistence. Talent will not; nothing is more common than unsuccessful men of talent. Genius will not; unrewarded genius is almost a proverb. Education will not; the world is full of educated derelicts. Persistence and determination alone are omnipotent".

A few minutes later, I almost shed tears of frustration and disappointment, when instead of the glass of milk I craved so much, I was handed a tin of condensed milk, an instance of unrewarded genius.

The local lads watched me as I eyed the tin and speculated on my next move. Had I followed my natural inclination, I would have thrown the tin at them.

I was still idly tossing the tin of milk from one hand to the other wondering what to do with it, when the house boy appeared with a jug of coffee, a cup and a tin opener.

Three cups of coffee laced with the tinned milk, which failed to destroy the delicious taste, appeased my protesting stomach.

With my energy partly restored, I decided to ask for a bath. This time my miming was understood. A single performance resulting in my being led to a hut which contained a brick receptacle about 5 feet square and 4 feet high filled with a filthy fluid, so repulsive looking, I refrained from even washing my hands, going to bed instead.

I must have slept until about 8 p.m. when the rest house keeper awakened me. His explanation needed no interpretation, he simply opened his mouth and pointed to it.

The food for dinner, which I devoured ravenously, was strange but quite edible and the coffee excellent. Although I drank a large quantity of this strong beverage, it did not prevent me from sleeping.

I was in bed again before 9 o'clock and after a good rest, up and waiting to be taken out to the aircraft well before 1.20 a.m.

The Malay driver made no excuse for turning up 20 minutes late. Time seemed to have no meaning for him. He was rather irritable, peevishly informing me that driving automobiles and aeroplanes should be confined to the hours of daylight.

We proceeded to the aerodrome at no more than 25 miles per hour, despite the driver's boast of yesterday to take me back to the aeroplane really fast.

I had little chance of finding the reason for his cautious behaviour, because he sounded the horn incessantly, although neither man nor beast was encountered en route. Perhaps the driver made the noise to give the impression he was driving fast, or maybe to scare the 'demons' away. Most unhappy, he dropped me hurriedly near the Swift and drove off without even a farewell wave.

After checking over the aircraft by the failing light of my torch and walking over the landing ground to see that there were no obstructions in the way of take off, I eventually got away at 2.50 a.m., climbing the Swift into a clear star studded sky, heading east.

Day dawned about two hours later turning the dark forbidding mountains of Flores into peaks of enthralling grandeur. This island must surely be one of the most beautiful on earth, with scenery so impressive I was sorry when Ambogaga, on the south coast appeared.

From here I headed the Swift out over the 168 miles of sea separating Flores from Timor. An hour and fifty minutes later the Swift was over Koepang and there was only one more sea to cross.

I came in over the town at 8,000 feet and by the time the Swift touched down on the aerodrome a mile or so to the east, a big fellow with a beard, a Turkish name and a good command of English was waiting to meet me.

As I stepped out of the aircraft, he ordered an assistant to refuel the Swift, then produced some food and coffee saying 'I expect you are in a hurry to get away'.

'Yes. But I want a bath first," I replied.

'You can get a bath in Darwin, the Turkish gentleman seemed to be in a hurry to get me away as soon as possible. 'You have no time to waste if you want to break the record'.

'The record will keep', I retorted. 'I haven't so much as washed my hands since leaving Batavia, I feel filthy'.

Many have remained unwashed for days and in the end may not have been much the worse for it. Nevertheless at the present moment, I felt more in need of a hot bath than anything else. Apart from the hygienic aspect, there is nothing more refreshing than a good soaking in hot water when one is sore and tired, nor any better boost for morale.

With ill grace, the Turk wasted no time taking me into Koepang, at high speed.

Two hours later, I was being driven back to the aerodrome at more than twice the 'really fast' speed the Malay had driven the Buick at Bima.

During those two hours I had had a glorious bath, shaved and put away an excellent breakfast, and now felt better than at any time since leaving England.

I had also spent some time studying the map covering the last stage to Australia, memorising features of the Australian coast on either side of Darwin, in the event of the weather being too rough for me to refer to the map when the Swift made landfall.

To make sure of setting out on the right course, I extended the track, already marked on the map, back over the west coast so that it would be possible to obtain an accurate orientation at the outset.

Before leaving England people had asked about my reaction concerning flying over the Timor Sea with an aircraft of such small capacity and the possibility of becoming lost.

At that time, at the other side of the world, the last stage to Australia seemed so remote, I did not give the matter much consideration. Now that the threshold of this stage had been reached, the idea of becoming lost never entered my head.

Although there was no way of telling whether the compass had deviated further since leaving Singapore, whether it would be necessary to detour around the storms predicted over the Australian side of Timor Sea (I had no intention of suffering a another repetition of the terrifying experience over the Java Sea), or whether a wind change of any magnitude would occur en route, I felt quite confident about reaching Darwin.

Thoughts of the dire result of an engine failure did cross my mind. Apart from the trouble approaching Basra, and that over the Adriatic, for which no blame could be attached to the engine, the behaviour of the Pobjoy had been faultless this far, so there was no logical reason for worrying about what might never happen over the comparatively short distance to Australia.

The wind was light and variable on the ground here, but on the journey from Bima the Swift had averaged no more than 92 miles per hour indicating that there had been head wind at 8,000 feet. Should similar conditions prevail over the Timor Sea the journey would take 5 hours 42 minutes.

On our way to the aerodrome the Turk asked what time I expected to arrive in Darwin. I told him the time I anticipated the journey to take and that the time of arrival depended on my departure from Koepang.

The Turk was silent for a few minutes, then he suddenly increased the speed of the car, already travelling too fast, in my opinion, until we were speeding along in such a dangerous manner, I had grave doubts about leaving Koepang, alive.

In response to my protest, the driver pointed out there was every need to hurry, concluding with the remark. "Twenty minutes is a very narrow margin. You wasted too much time in Koepang'.

Before I was able to ask for an explanation the car reached the aerodrome, pulling up alongside the Swift with screeching tyres. I was bustled out and as I donned my flying cap, the Turk pulled a huge bunch of bananas out of the back of the car and presented them to me, saying as be did so 'Kingsford Smith always takes a bunch of bananas with him to eat on the way, so I thought you would like some'.

I pointed out that not only would it be impossible to eat the bananas, there must have been at least a hundred of them, it would also be impossible for the Swift to carry such a load.

My Turkish friend wasted no time in disputing this, he plucked two bananas from the bunch thrusting them into my hands, and all but thrust me into the cockpit, his last words of farewell being 'You must break that record'.

His anxiety to speed my departure was very like that of Malony at Baghdad. Perhaps he, too, had made a wager on the outcome.

By ten o'clock the Swift was airborne, climbing away in the opposite direction of Darwin, soon to reach 4,000 feet, by which time it was well out over the sea.

Turning the aircraft through an 180° arc, I lined up on the point a little to the north of Koepang, where the track line to Darwin intersected the north west coast. Then setting the compass to a bearing on Cape Lewe, where the track crossed the coast on the far side of the island about 30 miles away.

On the first run over this course the Swift drifted gradually to the south. Taking the Swift back for another run, I reset the grid to allow for a 7° drift. Again the drift was slightly to the south. Edging the grid round another two degrees, I made the third attempt.

Spot on, the Swift crossed the coast over Cape Lewe. Orientation had taken approximately 20 minutes. So if the margin mentioned by the Turkish gentleman and my time estimate for the journey were correct, the Swift should arrive at Darwin having equalled the record. I wondered how that would affect the Turk's wager.

Making sure the Swift was on an accurate course at the start of the flight had been well worth the time and trouble, for it gave me a feeling of confidence about making a landfall in close proximity to Darwin.

Of course there was always the possibility of running into a thunderstorm. If such an event made it necessary to alter course I intended to make a change of 60° on every turn, carefully timing each deviation so that I could know, at all times the approximate position of the Swift in relation to the direct track, provided my mental arithmetic was able to cope with the effect of the wind. A problem to worry about if and when it occurred.

At present the day was perfect, with the air as calm as a mill pond, the sky cloudless and visibility unlimited.

The sun mounting towards its zenith, burnished the sea ahead with such brilliance, it dazzled the eyes. Not that this mattered, for most of the time I was concentrating on the compass needle lying parallel to the grid wires.

Flying in such conditions for any length of time, with no physical effort, there is always a danger of falling asleep unless the mind is actively occupied.

It was natural for my thoughts to be concerned with the young lady to whom I expected to plight my troth on the day after tomorrow and the problem of proceeding about this difficult and delicate matter.

I wondered if the shock would be too much for the lady when I swooped down from the sky and declared my intention of whisking her off to the altar at the earliest possible moment, and whether it would be wise to give warning of my intentions by sending the lady a telegram from Darwin. The idea of such an intimate communication being transmitted by strangers was not at all to my liking, yet what was I to do?

The solution to my problem would have been easy in prehistoric times, when a man simply clouted his beloved over the head with a cudgel, afterwards dragging her off to the love nest by the hair of her head but things were not so simple nowadays.

Since the fair sex had become emancipated, they had developed their own ideas regarding marital affairs and it seems in many instances I had seen it is they who do the courting. Verbally, of course. Many a stouter man than I had been rebuffed by that short and sour word 'No!'

This miserable and irresolute trend of thought I tried to dismiss by reviewing the performance of the Swift, by working out the amount of time taken to fly from England, this turned out to be exactly 100 hours by the time the aircraft was 35 minutes beyond Koepang. Next, I tried to calculate the number of revolutions the engine had completed during this period, a task which took some time. Then I tried to calculate the number of times the sparking plugs had fired, this proved too much for my mental capacity. It was a futile sort of exercise, but it certainly combated the hypnotic effect of gazing at the compass needle for so long.

My efforts to estimate the number of minutes elapsing before my arrival at Tooraweenah were interrupted when the Swift encountered slight turbulence.

Glancing out of the cockpit, I noticed the sea had become quite rough, the wind lanes on its surface indicating the wind had backed. Hoping the wind was constant up to this height, I altered course 5° to starboard.

Although two hours had elapsed since the departure from Koepang the time seemed to have passed quite quickly.

A number of pilots have been known to say that their lives in the air consist of long periods of boredom occasionally interspersed with moments of extreme tension. Exercising their brains when aloft would certainly offset their boredom, but it would be useless saying so to any of these pilots.

It was fruitless to offer advice to a fellow pilot unless he asked for it, because I have yet to meet an airman who did not think he was as good as, if not better than his fellow pilots.

I was beginning to think I was rather good myself. An opinion soon to be severely deflated.

Shortly after the wind change light cumulus cloud commenced forming and the clear cut horizon became obscured by haze. From this, an isolated build up of cu- nimbus appeared away to port, gradually absorbing its smaller cloud companions as it puffed out into the making of a heavy thunderstorm.

No more than 3 hours 32 minutes had elapsed since departure, when I thought I saw land about 20 miles away to the starboard.

To have crossed to Timor Sea in this time, the Swift would have to average about 160 miles per hour, an impossibility even if the wind had become a gale after changing direction.

Realising the sighting was a figment of my imagination, I resisted the temptation to change course towards the illusion. Several times I thought I had sighted land to one side or the other of the track, illusions I chose to ignore.

Then the engine coughed, causing my heart to leap in anticipation of worse to come, but the steady roar of the Pobjoy continued as if nothing had happened.

This fleeting incident rather upset me, and I wondered about the cause. The engine had barely exceeded its normal 100 hours period between overhauls and Doctor Pobjoy had assured me that it would be quite safe to run the engine for at least 130 hours before stripping it down.

A number of reasons could have caused the trouble, the most likely being a piece of carbon flaking off the cylinder head and jamming the inlet valve momentarily, or possibly it may have been just my imagination.

The cloud increased, some of it large cumulus, with a few thunderheads, fortunately well away from my track which remained clear although haze reduced visibility to within a few miles.

Four and three quarter hours after departure from Koepang, a lighthouse appeared out of the haze ahead. By the grace of God, I had made landfall at Point Charles, about two miles south of the direct track to Darwin. Ten minutes later the Swift touched down at Darwin.

The journey, so far, had been much slower than I had planned, nevertheless with only another 1,740 miles travelling to reach my objective, I should complete the journey within eleven days.

The Swift had barely rolled to a stop when a local character, fleet of foot. arrived alongside clutching a bottle of beer.

Whipping off the top he thrust the bottle at me, saying as he did so. "We've been keeping this on ice all day for you. I expect you could do with a drink, right now."

'Yes, but I'd rather have a cup of tea', I replied.

The man gave me look of surprise, tilted back his head and drank the contents of the bottle without pausing, wiping his mouth with the back of his hand, he commented. 'Well!, it takes all sorts to make a world'.

This performance had taken place so quickly it was all over before anyone else reached the aircraft.

The beer drinker vanished as suddenly as he had appeared, swallowed by the advancing crowd headed by my old friend, P. Allsop who happened to be in this part of the world, whilst on a business flight around Australia. With him was the Mayor of Darwin, Mr Brown who officially welcomed me.

What a contrast this was to the arrival at Bima where my welcome had been witnessed by a silent and orderly crowd. In Darwin many of those present were more interested in the Swift than the civic reception. They had probably heard Mr Brown speak on previous occasions and looked on me as a flying fool, lucky to arrive from overseas. The Swift was a different matter. None had seen an aircraft so small and many were the comments on this 'pint sized contraption', so termed by a local who stood at least 6 feet 3 inches in his boots.

Remarks about the Swift did not worry me, but when some of the crowd commenced see-sawing the ailerons, pulling the rudder and poking the fabric with their fingers, I became rather concerned, losing my composure completely as one youngster attempted to carve his initials on the side of the fuselage.

Fortunately the police took charge of the situation and moved the crowd away from the Swift whilst it was still airworthy.

'Slops' Allsop, one of the nicest men I knew, was so enraptured by the Swift, I invited him to fly the aircraft.

Well built and tall, Allsop had considerable difficulty settling into the cockpit which had been 'tailored' to fit my small, slim (126 lbs) figure. Spurred by facetious advice from the wags in the crowd, one of whom offered to fetch a shoehorn, 'Slops' was, eventually able to wriggle into a position where he could effectively handle the controls.

Once aloft, however, 'Slops' had no difficulty in giving a faultless flying exhibition. Skilfully demonstrating the wonderful manoeuvring ability of the Swift. A performance which thrilled the crowd, but caused me some worry, because I had forgotten to mention to 'Slops' that one of the engine bearers had been damaged.

'While Allsop was stirring up the atmosphere, the fleet- footed beer drinker returned with a billy of tea. Three cups of this, the best tea I had tasted since leaving England did much to banish my thirst and fatigue.

I was then interrogated by a friendly Customs Officer, who examined my documents, stamped my passport and asked if I had anything to declare.

I mentioned the alarm clock my aunt had given me and the flask of brandy presented by the lady at Rangoon. Both of these were 'souvenired' before I left Darwin.

The habit of souveniring indulged in by some Australians was beyond my comprehension, in the main things of no value except to the owner. A habit which had led to Australia being described as the land of the Bower Birds, some having wings and some having sticky fingers.

It was only with difficulty I restrained a young fellow from making off with my spare pair of goggles, which incidentally, disappeared a few days later, but I was unable to prevent a feminine filcher from snipping a button off my flying coat.

As soon as Allsop landed we were taken into town to pay our respects to the Administrator, followed by a call at the post office to send my parents a telegram notifying them of my arrival.

Here the Post Master surprised me by handing me a large sheaf of telegrams, saying as he did so. "I would also like to add my congratulations on breaking the record'.

'Did I break the record?' I asked. A question which caused some witticisms at my expense. I suppose it was rather stupid of me, but I had been too worried about the likelihood of the Swift being damaged by the crowd, to pay attention to the Mayor's welcoming speech at the aerodrome, and although a considerable number of people had grasped my hand remarking. "Well done'. "Goodonyermate', etc, etc, not one had mentioned anything about the record. Neither did the first half dozen telegrams I glanced at. Anyway it did not matter to me whether the record had been broken or not, my sole concern was for achieving my heart's desire.

The telegrams worried me though. Only 80 minutes had elapsed since my arrival, yet dozens of telegrams had arrived so far, if this spate of goodwill messages continued, it would be impossible for me to cope with replies. Acknowledging those I had just received would cost more than the few shillings remaining in my pocket. As for penning acknowledgements, the very idea appalled me.

When we arrived at the Victoria Hotel, Allsop and I were met by a deputation which requested us to attend a charity function being held that evening.

My pleas to be excused because I intended to leave Darwin at three o'clock tomorrow morning received little sympathy. Someone pointed out I could make a night of it and go straight out to the aerodrome from the dance. Which goes to show that these people either thought me a superman or just did not think at all. In the end we agreed to put in an appearance for half an hour. I then hastened to my room to see if the batch of telegrams, which I still clutched, contained one from my lady. There were telegrams from many parts of Australia, but none from Tooraweenah.

Had it not been for 'Slops' persuasion, I would have avoided the function to which we had been invited. Beside being dog tired, sore and sad, I looked like a tramp.

In urgent need of a haircut, with broken finger nails and garbed in oil-stained clothes, I was in no fit or proper state to attend a social gathering.

On arrival at the hall we were escorted to a platform and invited to be seated by a lady who seemed to be in charge of affairs.

Because of being seated for long periods in the cramped cockpit of the Swift, sitting had become so painful, I avoided doing so whenever possible.

Viewing with distaste my tardiness in becoming seated the lady repeated her request and when I said I would prefer to stand, advanced towards me and demanded. 'Why?'

My reply, spoken quietly, so I thought, was heard by several youngsters, who commenced tittering much to the annoyance of the lady, who led me to believe that she was under the impression I was an interloper, 'and unfit to be associated with the intrepid aviator ('Slops') who had recently reached our shores'. A natural impression for those who had come to the aerodrome after my arrival and had seen Allsop land after putting the Swift through its paces.

Leaving Allsop to face the music, I sneaked back to the hotel where I was appalled to find another batch of telegrams had been delivered by the post office people, who certainly provided the Darwin community with an excellent service.

Included in this batch was one from Tooraweenah, which considerably boosted my morale. Too excited to sleep, I brought my log books and diary up to date.

Without recording events soon after they had taken place it would have been impossible to have remembered all that occurred during the journey which so far had been entirely different from what I had imagined when planning my itinerary. Adverse weather on five of the nine days, although the Swift had been delayed no more than twice in this account.

The other five unexpected delays should never have occurred.

The behaviour of the Swift and its engine throughout the journey was astounding. Although the extreme variations of temperature, torrential rain, blasting dust and the sabotage at Naples had left their marks, the little aircraft was still flying as well as ever. Five hundred gallons of fuel had been consumed during the trip which had, so far, cost less than 100 pounds (including the cost of the maps). A splendid example of the development of aviation as a reliable and economic means of transport.

With the advantage of a far greater speed than any other means, it is clear that air transport will before long become predominant in the field of long distance travel.

For me the flight had been a satisfying and entertaining education, although at times very frustrating.

The awe inspiring weather encountered, glimpses of the strange countries en route and meeting with so many people of different race and outlook, brief though these meetings were, had broadened my vision and tempered my self esteem.

Three incidents remained enigmas to me. The mysterious happening over the Aegean Sea; the cause of the violent disturbance in the storm between Singapore and Batavia, both of which, I assumed, were due to unknown natural causes, and the wonderful exhilaration experienced on the flight between Jask and Karachi. An intangible feeling of being on the threshold of something greater than my mind could conceive. Something not conveyed by the normal senses, yet more stimulating than the sound of an enchanting melody, the sight of a glorious sunset, the delicate scent of a meadow at dawn, or the caress of a cool breeze on a hot day. A thrilling event etched deep on my memory.

My plan to leave Darwin at 3 a.m., have breakfast at Newcastle Waters, lunch at Camooweal and arrive at Longreach by sundown, went astray, because I did not awaken at the time intended, despite impressing on my mind when retiring, the time I hoped to awaken next morning, a method which on most occasions, proved satisfactory.

In addition to this habit, I had during the journey from England, set the alarm clock, as a further precaution, also whenever possible requested someone to awaken me. Only once, at Akyab, had these arrangements failed previously.

Unfortunately my alarm clock had been souvenired and the person who should have called me at 2 am failed to do so. I awakened eventually about 4.30 am, which coincidentally happened to be 2 am in Bima where I had spent the previous night.

Disillusioned by my mental 'timepiece' and annoyed about departing three hours later than planned, I took off from Darwin a few minutes before 6 o'clock, accompanied by Allsop as far as Pine Creek. Here 'Slops' headed for Wyndham, whilst I continued in a southeasterly direction over heavily timbered country, within gliding distance of the railway winding its way to Birdum.

A few minutes before ten o'clock, the Swift was abreast of Mataranka cattle station, ten miles away to the east, its landing ground a yellow slit in the green forest which stretched as far as the eye could see, in every direction.

I was tempted to drop in on Mr and Mrs Lowe for a cup of tea and would have done so had it not been for my yearning to reach Tooraweenah as quickly as possible.

Only a few months had passed since Mel Woodful, a cricket playing aviator, and I had spent several days at Mataranka homestead, rebuilding Reverend Langsford Smith's aircraft which had been damaged in a collision with an anthill on the edge of the narrow landing strip.

On that occasion the hospitality of the Lowes had been such, that we were both loth to leave when the job had been completed.

The sun climbed higher, and the temperature soared making flying at 3,000 feet so uncomfortable I took the Swift up to a cooler altitude.

At 8,000 feet visibility was perfect except for a slight dust haze on the horizon where the endless bush joined the sky.

As the Swift sped south the colour below gradually changed, the predominant tropical green becoming rather washed out. A country of controversy which was only fit for grazing cattle according to some people, others said it had great agricultural potentialities and that the Roper Valley alone could adequately support a couple of million people if wisely developed. Even if this intention is a trifle optimistic, it is not difficult to envisage this area, with its ample rainfall, becoming within 50 years or so, a civilised, closely settled farming region with its fields and orchards and prosperous townships.

Then the Swift was passing over Birdum, where the railway from Darwin terminated, but the ribbon of road continued stretching away over the southern horizon.

The Swift was making much better time at the higher altitude, speeding along in a manner reminiscent of my old pony which always made good time on the last stretch, homeward bound.

The timber below thinned, gradually giving way to patches of open country, Then the Swift was touching down at Newcastle Waters where I refuelled and ate a huge breakfast, kindly provided by the local policeman.

Fifty minutes later, I was on my way again after carefully orienting the Swift, as I had done when leaving Koepang. In addition to setting the compass, I picked three marks in line along the track and when over the nearest, selected another beyond the remaining two and so on. Although this method required considerable concentration, it is an accurate, though somewhat primitive, means of navigation and the best way of checking drift.

It was easy to get lost, as quite a number of aviators had done, over this isolated Barkly Tableland, where even a windmill is a welcome sight.

The road between Newcastle Waters and Camooweal was a mere track or rather a number of tracks meandering in so many directions they were useless for guidance.

After two and a half hours over this desolate country, where I sighted only one habitation and two windmills, I began to feel the effects of the journey. This was not surprising, considering I had had less than 27 hours sleep since leaving England ten days ago.

Only by rubbing my face vigorously, was I able to keep awake. The desire for sleep became so great by the time Brunette Downs came in sight, I decided to put the Swift down alongside the homestead and 'cadge' a cup of tea.

The Nelson's gave me a great welcome and several cups of tea. I felt sufficiently revived to continue on my way.

When Camooweal showed up nearly two hours after leaving Brunette the Swift had been in the air almost nine hours since leaving Darwin, almost as long as it had taken to fly from Bima to Darwin. With another 1,186 miles to travel to Tooraweenah, I realised, for the first time, what a large country Australia is.

Although Camooweal looked rather stark in the rays of the setting sun, I was very pleased to see it. In contrast to my arrival at Darwin, where a large, excited crowd had greeted me, here only a few goats witnessed my landing, avariciously eyeing the Swift through the fence which had been erected since my last visit, no doubt to prevent these destructive animals from devouring the fabric coverings of aircraft operating in this part of the world.

This settlement with it population of 300 people was unique in as much as it was the only country centre in Australia served by two airline companies. Qantas which operated a weekly service from Brisbane and Australian Aerial Services which ran a service across the Barkly Tableland to Daly Waters.

By the time I had tied the Swift to the fence and fitted the engine and cockpit covers, several small boys had joined the goats. They were intrigued by the Swift and its size and many questions were put to me about air speed, the horsepower of its engine, where had I come from and where I was going to, and had I ever flown a mail plane. This irritating inquisition was interrupted by the arrival of Alf Ashley and Bill Kirk, old colleagues of mine who ran the Daly Waters service, they took me into town after satisfying their curiosity about the Swift.

Only a few miles east of the dingo fence erected along the border between Queensland and Northern Territory and more than 100 miles from the nearest railway to which it is linked by an atrocious road, aptly named the 'springbuster', Camooweal is certainly a town in the outback, although not, as some say, 'at the back of beyond'. Yet! despite this isolation most of the local people are far from parochial. Nevertheless their outlook is different from the majority of Australians. For one thing they seemed more forthright and less emotional.

'Old man' Riley, the owner of the local hotel, for example, who on being told I had just flown in from England, said. 'So what! Did you expect him to be riding in on a horse? I told him he wouldn't stay long in that lousy, sunless hole.' He meant no offence. Flying to him was only a means of getting around. Had someone told him I had just arrived on a camel from Alice Springs or by bicycle from Sydney, his attitude would have been just as casual. He may have enquired about the weather in the Alice or Sydney, but not England, about which climate he seemed to have rather prejudiced views.

Just prior to leaving for England, I had ferried a D.H.50 aircraft from Melbourne to Camooweal. About this time the Australian currency had been devalued and was, so I had been told, no longer acceptable on board ship. Old Mr Riley, hearing me mentioning this to Alf Ashley, went to his till and sorting through his silver, produced about 30 shillings worth of English coins which he exchanged for Australian silver. He then suggested we go across to Synotts store.

Here the proprietor, who was busy, invited us to sort out the silver of his cash drawer, ourselves. This trust of strangers was indicative of the attitude of the people in those parts.

News of my quest spread rapidly, causing many of the towns people to search their bags and pockets for English coins so that before long I possessed most of the English silver in Camooweal.

With no bank within a hundred miles, ready cash, in this part of the country, sometimes became a problem, particularly to the storekeeper at times when the place was invaded by a stockmen and others, perhaps at the end of the season, when his till became full of cheques and devoid of cash.

This lack of money was overcome by the storekeeper issuing his own notes for change. I was told these notes, 'shinplasters' the locals termed then, circulated throughout an extensive area of this part of the outback, where the community assessed moral and material values by high standards which seem to be becoming unfashionable in the world of today, where honesty was regarded with great respect by the community in general.

After showering and swallowing a lemon squash, Ashley, Kirk and I returned to the aerodrome to refuel the Swift. Although adjacent to the settlement, the place was deserted except for the goats, still foraging in the vicinity.

Having in mind my experience at Darwin, I asked about a night watchman, Ashley assured me no one would think of touching the Swift, telling me that the whole of the time they had been operating at Camooweal not even a gallon of petrol had been stolen. Marauding animals had once been a bit of a problem, but the recent erection of the fence had stopped that.

Although 475 miles short of Longreach, which I should have reached that day I still reckoned on reaching Tooraweenah the following day. Departing from Camooweal at 4 o'clock in the morning and climbing to 10,000 feet, where the prevailing wind was westerly, I hoped to fly non-stop to Bourke, a distance of 920 miles.

Although the still air range of the Swift was only 849 miles, a tail wind component of 15 miles per hour would enable the Swift to reach Bourke with enough fuel for twenty minutes additional flying.

If the tail wind failed to materialize, I intended to land at Charleville or Cunnamulla to refuel. Such a diversion would extend the length of the trip, but I could still reach Tooraweenah the same day provided the weather remained fine.

The surface of several of the landing grounds en route had been far from good, but Camooweal aerodrome was certainly the worst so far as the Swift, with its small wheels, was concerned.

A small area was claypan, but most of the surface was black soil, often the bugbear of man and beast. When wet it becomes a glue, bogging all and sundry. When dry it cracks into unfathomable fissures sometimes more than a foot in width.

In dry windy weather, its fine particles become airborne filling the sky with a shroud sometimes so dark it is necessary to use lamps to see in the daytime. The deceptive appearance of its surface from the air has brought sorrow to many an aviator on landing and occasionally when taking off.

On arrival at Camooweal I had been able to land the Swift within the confines of the claypan. However, taking off with full load made it necessary to use all the space available, of which, at least 80% was black soil.

Shortly before 4 o'clock next morning, I was taxying the Swift across the aerodrome in the wake of a truck driven by Alf Ashley who had come to show me the best place for taking off.

The surface was very rough after the claypan had given way to black soil, where the going became so heavy it was necessary to open up the engine to nearly full throttle to keep the aircraft moving.

By the time the Swift was lined up for takeoff, I had become a trifle anxious about getting off such a rough ground in the dark.

While waiting for the dust, which had been stirred up by the two vehicles, to clear, I considered delaying departure until daybreak and if need be lighten the load by dumping some fuel. A delay which would have made it well nigh impossible to reach Tooraweenah the same day. However, the urgent desire to reach my goal overruled any caution I might have displayed in normal circumstances.

Wasting no time after the dust had cleared, I pushed the throttle as far as it would go. The Swift responded slowly, the black soil retarding its small wheels and making it difficult to keep the aircraft on a straight course until it had gathered sufficient speed for effective rudder control.

By then it seemed as if the Swift had covered the greater part of the aerodrome. In the dark it was impossible to tell distance run, and I was beginning to regret not waiting for Ashley to drive the truck to the far end of the ground to give some indication of the run available, when the Swift became airborne.

As I heaved a sigh of relief at successfully negotiating the roughest takeoff experienced so far, the nose suddenly dipped and veered to the right. I quickly corrected this unusual movement and the Swift climbed away in normal manner.

Although there had been no sound of the impact, it was obvious the Swift had struck an obstruction soon after leaving the ground. Probably an animal had somehow managed to get to the aerodrome and being disturbed by the noise of the aircraft, had run before it until being overtaken and struck a glancing blow by the starboard wheel.

The intrusion of animals on landing grounds often caused alarming incidents and quite a few accidents. Humans, horses, and dogs frequently offended in this respect during the brief though critical periods of landing and takeoff when the ability to manoeuvre an aircraft is rather restricted.

Previously, I had been involved in a few incidents of this nature and had witnessed several others.

On this last occurrence, the aircraft had apparently escaped damage. All the controls seemed to be functioning normally and the engine was running as smoothly as ever which meant the propeller had not been involved.

Owing to darkness, it was impossible to set an accurate course for Bourke, the compass being in the condition it was, so I headed the Swift in the direction of Cloncurry, intending to set course direct for Bourke, from there, or if the Swift had made slow time from Camooweal, to Charleville.

In less than 20 minutes the Swift had climbed to 10,000 feet and 25 minutes later a subtle change in the eastern sky, heralded the dawn.

Daylight came quickly, disclosing Mount Isa about 10 miles away on my right. The Swift was a few miles off the direct course to Cloncurry, but it was averaging at least 130 miles per hour, carried along by a strong tail wind which if it continued would enable me to reach Bourke will before midday.

Between England and Australia the wind had seldom been favourable, in fact, the flight had taken four hours longer than it would have done if the air had been calm throughout the journey.

Now for the last lap, providence had graced me with the gift of a gale on my tail. I was quite elated when the Swift reached Cloncurry 70 minutes after departure, averaging about 145 miles per hour. Provided this speed could be maintained the Swift would be abreast of Bourke by 10.15a.m., and have no trouble in reaching Tooraweenah without refuelling.

When I poked my head over the side to pinpoint my position precisely to orient the aircraft on course for Tooraweenah, I was astonished to find the starboard wheel was missing. Quickly I looked over the other side, where the port wheel was spinning slowly in the slipstream. Unable to believe my eyes, I glanced again over the starboard side, the wheel was certainly missing, not only that, the whole of the starboard side of the under carriage had disappeared, probably draped on the posterior of a dead goat or horse at Camooweal.

My joyful anticipation of reaching Tooraweenah vanished, to be instantly replaced by apprehensive perplexity. It was hard to realise that half the undercarriage had been torn from the Swift so quietly and without more serious consequences to the aircraft.

There had been no indication of an impact great enough to wrench off the undercarriage. The Swift had certainly behaved abnormally just after takeoff, but its unusual movement had not been severe and had been easily corrected.

The noise of the engine running at full throttle may have drowned the sound of the radius rod, axle and shock strut being ripped from the aircraft, but why I had not felt the shock of this happening was beyond my comprehension.

Conjecture was futile. The only thing to do now was to think of a way to get out of this invidious situation with as little damage as possible to myself and the aircraft. It was obvious that the next landing would be the last the Swift would make, at least, for some time.

Should I be fortunate enough to land without much further damage, the starboard side of the undercarriage would have to be rebuilt, and the missing wheel, which had probably escaped damage, found and forwarded on.

The question was, should I continue on my way hoping to reach Tooraweenah, a course that depended on the Swift maintaining its present ground speed.

Considering its vagaries, the wind was quite likely to peter out before my destination was reached, forcing me to land at Bourke. Should this happen I could reach Tooraweenah, by train and coach, probably the day after tomorrow. That is if I was able to land without injuring myself. This of course would mean abandoning the Swift, which I was loth to do.

On the other hand I could chance a landing at Cloncurry have the remains of the undercarriage brought from Camooweal by Qantas and attempt to rebuild it in a local garage.

The idea of returning to Camooweal occurred to me, but I was afraid of landing on the rough ground.

Then I thought of Longreach where Qantas had established workshops. There was no better place for major repairs. Even if I wrecked the Swift when landing, Qantas would have the facilities to rebuild the aircraft.

My morale took a slightly upward trend as I turned the Swift on course for Longreach, over country so familiar to me, reference to the compass was unnecessary. Nevertheless, I was worried about the effect this mishap would have on the outcome of my mission. It would be heartbreaking if I failed because of the lengthy delay which must ensue as the result of this accident.

Longreach was over 300 miles away, so there was plenty of time to consider ways and means of landing the Swift with as little damage as possible.

First essential was to use all the fuel before attempting a landing. Apart from the danger of fire, it was necessary for the Swift to be as lightly laden as possible, to reduce stalling speed to a minimum.

At the present time, the tanks held approximately 35 gallons, sufficient for nearly seven hours more flying. This would take nearly seven hours more to exhaust, by then I would be tired and probably incapable of successfully making a good landing of the crippled aircraft during the heat of the day, when the stalling speed would be greater than during the early morning.

About 20 gallons remained in the auxiliary tank after filling the main tank as the Swift approached Cloncurry. If this could be jettisoned, the fuel remaining would be exhausted 20 minutes after arriving over Longreach, enabling a landing to be made about 8.15 am.

I thought of getting a spanner from the tool kit in the head rest to uncouple the pipe connection at the hand pump then pump the fuel out of the auxiliary tank into the cockpit. The possibility of being overcome by petrol fumes made me decide against this idea.

The only other means of jettisoning was by pumping from the auxiliary to the main tank from which the fuel would overflow through the 1/8" diameter air vent. Although a very slow process, this would shorten the time in the air considerably, if I started the job immediately.

Soon a fuel trail was streaming back over the centre section, so thin it could hardly be seen.

A few minutes later the engine commenced running unevenly, then it suddenly misfired and almost jumped out of the aircraft as it misfired again.

Mindful of the damaged engine bearer, I throttled back quickly and scanned the ground below for a likely place to land.

Landing the heavily laden Swift, with a sound undercarriage, even on rough ground presented no great problem, but under the present circumstances, I had considerable doubt about 'walking away' from the landing I was about to make.

From this height (10,000 feet), the dark grey earth, etched with many dry creeks running from southwest to northeast and liberally spotted with scrub, reminded me of the lines and blotches on a sunburned face of an old bushman. Without sight of any human habitation, it looked a most unfriendly frowning land.

Seconds ticked by, whilst the Swift, silent except for the whistle of the slipstream, glided eastward and earthward.

In vain I searched for somewhere to put the Swift down without too much damage. From 4,000 feet the features of the ground were quite distinct, but looked hopeless for landing.

'Oh why. Oh why did the engine have to die over such a spot?' The sound of my voice startled me. Normally I was not given to asking myself inane questions or talking to myself for that matter.

My acute stress was relieved a few seconds later by the McKinley track showing up ahead, where it doglegged a mile or so before crossing the Hamilton River. The glare of the sun had prevented me from seeing it earlier.

With the aid of the tail wind it looked as if the Swift might just reach the road and even if wrecked on landing, at least I had a chance of being picked up by some traveller during the day.

At a thousand feet the wind apparently died and it became obvious the Swift, unable to reach the track, would crash on the rough ground between.

In desperation, I opened the throttle. Matters could not be much worse should the engine bearer collapse. The engine coughed and spluttered a few times, then ran smoothly, so I pushed the throttle forward to cruising position.

The Swift held height at about 200 feet as it came over the track which appeared so rough it would have been impossible to have put the aircraft down, with its damaged undercarriage, without breaking, it up.

I took the Swift back to 10,000 feet wondering what had caused the engine to fail, and then came alive again when it was urgently needed.

At the end of the climb, I recommenced jettisoning the fuel. Soon the engine commenced to misfire again, I immediately closed the throttle and ceased pumping, realising the excessive pressure in the main tank was causing the trouble.

The air vent being too small to discharge the fuel as fast as it was delivered had resulted in such a build up of pressure in the main tank it was upsetting the carburation. Thereafter I took care to keep the pressure within bounds whilst maintaining a constant discharge from the vent.

The Swift was less than 160 miles from Longreach when the last of the fuel was pumped from the auxiliary tank, not that distance mattered now. With fuel remaining for approximately 3 hours flying, the chronological factor was now paramount. The time of 9.54 am to be precise, the moment I expected the fuel to run out.

Jettisoning as much fuel as possible had reduced by over two hours the time the Swift would have to remain aloft.

Apart from being able to land before the hottest part of the day, the reduction in the time of waiting for the critical moment to arrive would relieve, to a certain extent, the mental stress as well as the fatigue from which I suffered more and more each day, towards the end of the flight.

At 7 o'clock when Winton came in sight, a few miles away on the left, it was evident the Swift was making the fastest speed over the ground since leaving England, a ridiculous state of affairs, since speed was now of no consequence. It was also tantalizing to realise the Swift may have reached Tooraweenah non-stop.

The Swift arrived over Longreach a few minutes before 8 o'clock with enough fuel for two more hours flying. Having to loiter around the sky for another hour tempted me to essay a landing as soon as possible. The scent of frying bacon, which my imagination conjured up, was an added inducement to get down to earth.

As the aircraft lost height, circling over the town, I considered the problems of putting the Swift down as gently as possible under the circumstances. Finally deciding to land across wind, tail down with the port side to windward and the port wing as close to the ground as possible. If this position could be held until most of the speed was lost, the wind resistance on the side of the fuselage would, to a certain extent, counteract the tendency to ground loop, when the unsupported starboard wing hit the ground.

By the time the Swift had circled down to 3,000 feet, it had been joined by several hawks. One or two of the boldest coming much too close for my peace of mind.

Down on the aerodrome, the windsock hanging limp; still as the post to which it was attached, indicated a dead calm on the ground despite the strong wind aloft.

Realising the weight of the fuel remaining in the tank situated well above the centre of gravity of the aircraft and the calm conditions, would increase the risk of the Swift turning over on landing, I decided to curb my impatience and stay aloft, as I had originally intended, until the fuel was exhausted, hoping a breeze would spring up meanwhile.

After flying over the town and aerodrome for my plight to be seen, I climbed to a safer height to write a note to the Qantas people telling them of my intention to stay aloft until the fuel had been used and the estimated time of landing.

Writing the message on one of the leaves of the customs carnet, the only thing available, was not easy in the cramped cockpit, but the brief note was legible. Unfortunately there was nothing at hand to weight the message, which would most likely float away into the 'never never' once it was cast into the slipstream, so I took the Swift down to within 100 feet of the aerodrome, tossing the note overboard in front of the Qantas hangar, then circling to observe the result.

Several boys were weaving an erratic course across the aerodrome in pursuit of the floating paper and great activity was taking place in front of the hangar. Then I recognised Lester Brain staggering on to the tarmac carrying a wheel on his right shoulder. My plight had been observed.

185

Much as I appreciated old Lester's (I always thought of Lester as being old. Although he was no older than I, he seemed much more dignified and mature, by my reckoning) action warning me of my predicament, I could not help being amused by what seemed to me, to be the time, a very comical act.

As the sun climbed higher so did the temperature, making flying uncomfortable near the ground where it was hot and the air bumpy.

Before going up to a cooler altitude, I made several runs across the aerodrome to select the best place for putting the Swift down, afterwards climbing to 6,000 feet to await the exhaustion of the fuel.

Down below a constant stream of cars and pedestrians were making their way to the aerodrome. News of my peril was spreading fast.

It is unusual to have prior notice of an aeroplane accident, such incidents generally occur without warning, more often than not in some out of the way spot. For such a happening to take place on their front doorstep, so to speak, seemed to be appreciated by many of the local citizens, judged by the crowd gathering below.

Time dragged on seemingly slower and slower, whilst I tried to keep my mind from dwelling on the ordeal ahead of me. Having considered the problem from every angle and decided on a definite plan, it would be futile to reiterate the subject and probably confuse the issue.

I tried to turn my thoughts to the past, (contemplation of the future would have been tempting providence), by recalling previous incidents of a similar nature. The time when a dog, disputing my right of way when I was taking off at Cootamundra, had been skittled for its pains and the horse, which racing across the front of the aircraft as I was about to touch down at Cowra, had received a hefty clip on the ear. Neither the animals nor the aircraft had suffered, but my nerves had been somewhat frayed by these incidents.

Not so S. E. Sutcliffe who piloting a D.H.50 on its final approach at Hay when, unseen by the pilot because of the restricted view from the cockpit of this type, a grazing horse, wandering into the path of the approaching aircraft, had been smacked on its posterior with such force, it was pitched on to its head, the aircraft speeding over the prostrate animal, quickly disappearing into a cloud of dust as it touched down.

The horse staggered to its feet, whipping round to face its adversary, seeing nothing to account for its discomfiture, it kicked its heels in the air, snorted, and seemingly none the worse for its encounter galloped away before the D.H.50 reappeared out of the dust, its pilot puzzled by the lack of evidence of the incident which he had heard but not seen.

These incidents occurred less frequently now, because the authorities were fencing landing grounds. However it was still necessary to carefully examine an aerodrome before landing.

Rabbits seemed to delight in producing burrows on some country aerodromes, particularly those well grassed. A condition which also tempted some stockowners when fodder was short elsewhere, to open gates of aerodromes infrequently visited by aircraft.

Shortly after nine o'clock, quite a number of cars which had been lining the aerodrome boundary, started moving back to town, the occupants, probably, having more important things to do than watch an aircraft circling in company with a flock of hawks. Even the birds, their curiosity satisfied so far as the Swift was concerned, eventually moved over the far side of the town in search of more palatable prey.

By the time the clock on the dash showed 11.30 G.M.T (9.30 am local time), it was no longer possible to think of anything but the immediate future.

The last drop of fuel was due to run out within 24 minutes, thus beginning what might be the Swift's last glide. As the minute hand moved imperceptibly towards the crucial moment, my imagination began to play havoc with my logic. My mind picturing being dragged from a wrecked aircraft, suffering from a broken nose, a pair of black eyes and an ear torn off, to say nothing of mangled limbs and the liberal quantity of gore spilled.

Then the crisis was at hand. Like a runner on the blocks awaiting the crack of the starter's pistol, I tensed, watching the second hand making its journey round the clock to complete that last vital minute, and waiting for the noise of the engine to cease.

Maybe it was expecting too much for the petrol consumption calculations to be absolutely precise despite the care taken in this respect, but when an additional five minutes had elapsed without any sign of the engine faltering, the absurd idea occurred that the engine would continue for evermore. Sixty-five seconds later the engine coughed and spluttered, picked up and ran for a few more seconds as I put the nose down, finally fading away, leaving an uncanny silence, broken only by the wind whistling past the struts.

With the sin of waiting over, my faculties returned to normal. Switching off the ignition, I held the nose of the Swift up until the propeller ceased revolving. Unfortunately the blades stopped in an almost vertical position. Diving the aircraft until the propeller started revolving, I again pulled up the nose. A manoeuvre which had to be repeated several times before the blades were horizontal, a position least likely for them to be damaged should the Swift nose over after landing.

'Dead stick' approaches and landings are not difficult provided the pilot knows the 'feel' of the aircraft and care is taken during descent to see that the final approach can be made into wind on to the spot selected. The descent made a fraction above stalling to prevent the propeller from windmilling, was quite leisurely and uneventful until the noise of a car being started up suddenly, seemingly only a few yards away, startled me so much I almost stalled the aircraft.

Then I heard the bark of a dog and other sounds to be expected in and around a town. That these sounds should carry so high and with such clarity rather surprised me.

Below two thousand feet the draft slackened making it easier for me to put the Swift down in the way I hoped. At 1,000 feet the Swift was heading south a few yards beyond the western boundary of the aerodrome and by the time I had swung the aircraft round facing a few points east of north it was down at 400 feet and losing height fast. The southern boundary slipped by about 80 feet beneath as I skidded the aircraft round until it was about 45° out of wind, which was so slight, drift was imperceptible.

Six feet from the ground the aircraft was horizontal and I started to bring the tail and port wing down. A few inches above the surface, the Swift floated seemingly reluctant to leave the air, its port wing skimming along with no more than a foot to spare.

Eventually the port wheel and skid touched, 'light as a kiss of an angel' and the Swift slowed quickly on the soft dark grey soil, the port wing coming up above the horizontal as the starboard wing dropped to the ground, swinging the Swift to the right as it came to a stop.

By the grace of God, no further damage had been done, so far as I could tell.

Lester Brain, approaching much faster than his usual dignified gait, was first to greet me. 'Well done', he said, which was quite a compliment from Lester.

Dudley Wright, the next to arrive welcomed me with. 'What the bloody hell do you think you're up to?'. Dudley and I were old friends, having shared the trials and tribulations of the bad old days as engineers with Australian Aerial Services at Hay.

For an aircraft to be damaged, no matter the reason, was sacrilege in Dudley's eye and he was never one to beat about the bush concerning such matters.

Before I could think of a fitting reply, a fellow pushed Dudley aside and insisted on shaking my hand, saying as he did so. 'That was a mighty job you did mate. Made me a packet you have'. Before I could ask for an explanation for this puzzling statement, the fellow disappeared. I was told later he was a bookmaker who, to while away the time while I was circling overhead, had made wagers, with some of the local lads on the various amounts of damage the Swift and I might sustain when landing. A macabre manner to fill in time. Yet, I am sure, had I come to grief, the punters or whatever they are termed would have been as dismayed as I.

Despite escaping without a scratch, I got out of the Swift feeling rather depressed, until I saw the remains of the starboard undercarriage jammed beneath the fuselage and attached to it by a single bolt.

The axle and wheel seemed to be alright, but the radius rod and shock strut with their attachment fittings were damaged beyond repair.

No time was lost in taking the crippled Swift over to the Qantas hangar where it was jacked on trestles so that an exact assessment could be made of the damage. The starboard wheel and tyre were in good condition and so was the axle except for an elongated bolt hole which could be repaired. The remainder of the undercarriage and its attachment fittings would have to be replaced.

Fortunately Qantas had the raw material for manufacturing the new parts.

The only damage sustained during the landing had been caused by the starboard wheel loosening the fabric covering beneath the fuselage and a small hole in the fabric of the starboard wing where it dragged on the ground.

Less than three hours after my arrival the damaged fittings had been removed from the machine and templates draughted and made for the new fittings, from then on until the repairs were completed next day, my recollection of events is very hazy, except that by 2 p.m on Thursday, the Swift was back on its wheels looking as good as new.

That so much work could have been done, so well, in so short a time, seemed incredible. Nic Comper, I am sure, would have been delighted to see Dudley Wright and his colleagues tackling this job.

Without drawings it is no easy matter to produce a number of components, the final assembly of which must be accurate for the undercarriage to function properly.

I have no memory of whether any of us ate or slept during the 28 hours it had taken to do the work, but when it had been completed and the Swift wheeled on to the tarmac, I discovered I was too exhausted to fly the aircraft, wisely deciding to postpone my departure until next day.

One of the men who had worked so hard on the Swift, was rather upset when he learned about the postponement. He tried to persuade me to wait until Saturday before leaving Longreach, because he was afraid - so he said - that I would meet with a sticky end if I flew the next, Friday - the 13th.

I suspected a 'leg pull', but when this Job's comforter turned up at the aerodrome at five o'clock next morning and tried again to dissuade me from flying that day, I was rather perturbed. Not that his premonition worried me, but I disliked offending this fellow, by ignoring his plea, because he had worked so hard on the Swift.

The ensuing dialogue delayed the takeoff so that it was 5.40 a.m. before the Swift was airborne and heading for Charleville across the scrub strewn plains, golden tinted by the rays of the early morning sun and slashed by the occasional bore drain.

It had been my intention to fly direct to Tooraweenah, but invitations had come from Charleville, Bourke and Nyngan to call on the way south. Although this would delay my ultimate arrival by several hours, it would have been unkind to deny my friends in these places the opportunity of seeing the Swift.

Although the sky was clear and the air calm, I was unable to enjoy the perfect weather conditions, because of the pain from my nether regions, caused by being confined to an immovable position which restricted the circulation of blood.

This trouble had become progressively worse as the journey proceeded, but hitherto my hind quarters had become so numbed, after I had been in the air for a while, no pain was felt until the circulation returned after landing.

Today the pain persisted, maybe, because of the spell from flying during the preceding two days.

Charleville showed up after I had been in the air for a little over two hours, by then I was almost howling with the pain.

Despite the early hour a large crowd had gathered when the Swift touched down at 7.50 am. The Mayor and George Herriman of Qantas were first to greet me, then my hand was being shaken by the townsfolk until my arm ached almost as much as my backside.

This ordeal lasted forty minutes, then, not waiting for breakfast, I fled to Bourke, where the ground was shimmering in a temperature of 90°, when I landed alongside the railway station a few minutes before eleven o'clock.

Immediately on arrival I was taken to Ken Fitzgerald's hotel for a civic reception and refreshments. A couple of thousand words, 3 cups of tea and 20 minutes later I was aloft again bound for Nyngan.

Although 85% of the country between Bourke and Nyngan is covered with the thick shrub so menacing to aviators, the Department of Civil Aviation had cleared emergency landing grounds at intervals of 20 miles or so, along and adjacent to the railway which ran straight as a plumb line between the two towns, a route that even the inexperienced pilot could confidently fly over in all sorts of conditions, excepting a severe dust storm.

In fact, compared with what I had seen overseas, Australia was well to the fore so far as aviation generally is concerned.

My old friend Albert Priest and the Mayor Charles O'Reilly, who had known me since my childhood, met me on my arrival at Nyngan, where the mayor supported by another worthy citizen welcomed me officially. Their eulogy and the approbation of the crowd, naturally affected my ego. I was beginning to believe in the flattery to which I had been subjected since my arrival in Darwin. That my prowess as an aviator, my courage and my endurance were outstanding.

This mental adulation was, however, severely deflated by memory of the narrow escape I had had at Camooweal, where the Swift had collided with the fence, not a straying animal as I had thought.

The knowledge that I had been culpable made me feel rather uncomfortable as I listened to the mayor extolling my virtues.

Of course, I could salve my ego at the expense of my conscience by blaming the shortcoming of Camooweal aerodrome regarding its length, its rough surface and lack of lighting, or even my fatigue for causing the accident, but that would only be self-delusion.

Flying an aeroplane is a simple matter, so simple indeed, a child of twelve could be taught to fly within a few hours. No special talent, nor abnormal physical or mental qualifications are required to become a competent pilot. The ease with which many pilots learn to fly, gives some a false sense of security, a feeling that they are 'Lord of the Sky' immune from harm. An attitude which can and sometimes does lead to disastrous consequences. These consequences, often head- lined by the press, have given many people the impression that flying is a hazardous occupation requiring great courage and extraordinary endeavour.

This worthy citizen of Nyngan was apparently one of these people, for many were the embellishments this well meaning man employed to my embarrassment. Perhaps skill and courage are required to fly an aeroplane, but these attributes are of little value without care and caution.

The end of the speeches brought another ordeal. The crowd surged forward and soon my right hand and arm were in such a sorry state from being shaken it seemed likely I would be forced to fly the Swift, left handed on the final stage.

I managed to escape eventually, getting the Swift airborne and heading east, with a feeling of relief which changed to exuberance as the jagged peaks of the Warrumbungles came up over the horizon, nearly a hundred miles away. Soon the whole of the rugged range was revealed, an impressive massif rising out of the plains to a height of well over 3,000 feet.

These mountains - the oldest in the world according to some geologists - smoky green, topped with gold by the westering sun, provided a magnificent spectacle as they expanded with my approach.

Mount Exmouth, The Bluff and the Spire, gigantic chunks of rock, green skirted with bushland, dominated the scene which gradually changed as the plains, scattered with scrub, gave way to fields of ripening wheat stretching away to the Warrumbungles, where Tooraweenah nestles in the western foothills, its inhabitants as yet, unaware their peace and quiet was soon to be shattered by the roar of the Swift.

Across the railway along which a goods train was puffing its way south from Coonamble and on over the Castlereagh River, devoid of surface water, the Swift sped towards its goal, which appeared a few minutes later looking like Lilliput from 4,000 feet.

A sight more thrilling to me than the first glimpse of the lighthouse on Point Charles.

Having reached my destination, the temptation to indulge in a display of aerobatics was hard to resist, instead I gradually closed the throttle and made a sedate descent. The Swift, beside the onslaught of the elements, had suffered enough at my bands during its brief existence.

It was remarkable that a few planks of wood, a roll of fabric, some brass tacks, a coil or two of wire, several pints of dope, a few ounces of glue, plus several pounds of metal had been fashioned into this wonderful machine which had carried me half round the world; all within a month.

As the Swift lost height over the village, I looked for a suitable landing place. There being no landing ground at Tooraweenah, I had on previous occasions landed in a variety of places. Shumack's paddock where I had landed on my first visit, was covered with a crop of ripening wheat. Another place, I had used, the lane at the back of the village, the wheel tracks were too deep for putting the Swift down safely, and farther out grazing stock were scattered about Yeo's paddock.

The village itself is divided by a tree lined creek spanned by an old wooden bridge carrying the road linking the old and the new parts of the settlement.

South of the creek, the post office, police station, bank and public hall were clustered, with the 'pub' and a few houses a short distance away. The show ground and football field in the outskirts - there was no suitable landing place here.

Across the creek the road which sloped uphill to the northwest for about 70 yards to the older part of the village where the general store, a couple of cottages and the home of the lady, stood on one side, facing the school, the church and a few more houses on the other. Here the road ran straight and level for at least 150 yards before winding over a hill to Coonamble.

It was on this stretch I decided to put down the Swift. It seemed appropriate to land alongside the front doorstep of the lady and say I had dropped in to ask her to marry me. But that was not to be.

After flying down low over the places to make sure there were no meandering dogs or fowls in the vicinity, I banked the Swift for the final approach and was about to sideslip down over the trees lining the creek, intending touch down on the crest of the slope, when a mob of children erupted from the school on to the road in front of the approaching Swift, forcing me to open up the engine and climb away.

Other than Yeo's paddock, all the other likely landing places within reasonable distance of Tooraweenah, were under crops. Either I had to search further afield or attempt a landing on Alf Yeo's property with the risk of skittling one of his cows.

Choosing the latter, I selected a gap between the grazing animals, bringing the Swift to its final landing without so much as a glance from the browsing beasts.

By the time I had taxied the Swift to the lee of a hay stack where I intended to tie it down, (as a precaution against the katabatic wind which, even on a calm night, is liable to roar down suddenly from the mountains with the speed of an express train, turbulent enough to overturn an aircraft not firmly secured) numerous youngsters fleet of foot and untrammelled by dignity arrived and stood talking and giggling, watching me while I slapped my buttocks and stamped my feet to restart the blood circulating to my nether regions as I, eager for the sight of the lady watched dust rising along the back from the village, heralding the approach of several cars. My head full of fond and fine words of greeting.

Then the lady was before me, and I, entranced by her radiance, was able to utter nought but a mundane 'Hello'.

Nevertheless, my flight to a lady had not been in vain!.

Authors note

The inexplicable happenings mentioned earlier are no longer mysterious. Ice accretion on the wings probably caused the incidents over the Aegean and the violent behaviour of air currents in severe thunderstorms is now common knowledge. The exhilaration experience on the flight between Jask and Karachi could have resulted from lack of oxygen whilst flying at a comparatively high altitude for such a lengthy period.

C. A. Butler
8/6/68

Doris Garling, c.1931.

Doris and Arthur on front lawn of Doris's family home, Tooraweenah, c.1931.

Author in flight over countryside.

Author inspecting engine at an unknown location.

Royal Aero Club aerodrome at Hargreave Park.
The Comper-Swift was the first overseas aircraft
to land there on 15th November, 1931.

Mr. J. Oak-Rind, Director of Vacuum Oil Co. Pty Ltd., presenting C. A. Butler
with a model of the Comper-Swift monoplane in which the latter created
a new record of 9 days, 1 hour, 43 minutes from England to Australia.
Sir Charles Kingsford-Smith on right.

Comper Swift outside Garling's store,

Tooranweenah Aerodrome. Butler Air Transport Heron in foreground.

Patient being transferred to Butler plane at Tooraweenah.

www.ingramcontent.com/pod-product-compliance
Lightning Source LLC
Chambersburg PA
CBHW070954040426
42443CB00007B/507